Building
a Better World

Building a Better World

A Contemporary Augustinian Perspective

Arthur Purcaro, O.S.A.

Foreword by
Pope Leo XIV

Published in the United States by New City Press
136 Madison Avenue, Floors 5 & 6, PMB #4290
New York, NY 10016
www.newcitypress.com

© 2026 Arthur Purcaro, O.S.A.

Excerpts from the Rule of St. Augustine, with Introduction and Commentary by T. J. Van Bavel, O.S.A., translated by Raymond Canning, O.S.A., ©1984 Darton, Longman, & Todd. Used with permission.

Cover and interior paintings by the author.
ISBN: 978-1-56548-730-7 (Paperback)
ISBN: 978-1-56548-731-4 (E-book)

Printed in the United States of America

Contents

Foreword (by Pope Leo XIV) 7
Preface 9
General Introduction 13
    Integral Ecology 15
    Saint Augustine 19
    The Choir 22
    The Temple 23
    The Augustinian Order 24
    Communal Holiness: Living in Harmony 26
    Augustine and the Environment 27

Love Is the Essential Nucleus 35

    Opening Exhortation of *The Rule of Augustine* 35

The Ideal Toward Which We Strive: Harmony 41

    Setting the Scene: A Christmas Vignette 41
    The Rule of Augustine, Chapter 1 42
    What Is Meant by Material Poverty? 45

The Practice of Prayer in Common 51

    Another Vignette to Set the Scene on This Topic 51
    The Rule of Augustine, Chapter 2 52

Living Simply, in Harmony, to Share 60

    Setting the Scene with Another Vignette:
    Petronila of Pacaipampa 60

The Rule of Augustine, Chapter 3 61
What a Waste! Live Simply in Order to Share 69

Mutual Responsibility for Growing in Harmonious Living 71

The Rule of Augustine, Chapter 4 73
What Is Fraternal Correction? 79
Points Made by Saint Augustine Regarding
Fraternal Correction: 80

Serving the Greater Good Through the Communion of Goods 86

Another Vignette to Introduce Us to the Call to Conversion 86
The Rule of Augustine, Chapter 5 88

Forgiving One Another 97

A Vignette to Situate the Topic of This Chapter 97
The Rule of Augustine, Chapter 6 98
Another Vignette Might Help Grasp the Significance of
Forgiving from the Heart 105

Responsible Authority Through Listening and Love 109

Another Vignette to Help Situate the Topic of This Chapter 109
The Rule of Augustine, Chapter 7 111

Concluding Exhortation: The Gracious Gift of Fidelity 119

Nature as Mirror: A Vignette to Situate the Topic of
the Final Chapter of *The Rule* 119
The Rule of Augustine, Chapter 8 120

Call to Action 129

Appendix: The Rule of Saint Augustine, complete text 133

Foreword

Saint Augustine reflects upon the power of words and on the importance of the word as the vehicle that communicates truth to others. In Sermon 293, he writes: "Note that if I think of what I am going to say, the word already exists in my heart. But if I want to speak to you, I am concerned to render present to your heart what is already present in mine."

Father Art Purcaro, in this book on *The Rule of Saint Augustine*, has succeeded in communicating what he has held in his heart for many years, as an Augustinian, priest, missionary, and especially as a disciple of Jesus. Art Purcaro now offers to his readers some of the fundamental principles that continue to guide men and women throughout the world as they seek to follow the Gospel in the spirit of Augustine. And he then takes the additional step of demonstrating how that spirituality and lifestyle continue to offer a vital message to all of us today.

The particular perspective that Fr. Purcaro takes in this reflection on *The Rule of Saint Augustine* is expressed in the title he has given to the book: *Building a Better World: A Contemporary Augustinian Perspective*. Augustine's *Rule*, written almost 1600 years ago, continues to offer a living spirituality that is of meaning and value in our own times.

As the Church celebrates the tenth anniversary of the Encyclical Letter *Laudato si'*, it is more than appropriate to point out that Pope Francis clearly recognized the deep relationship between living human relationships (important for Augustine, as we see clearly throughout *The Rule*) and the care of the gift of creation. In number 226 of *Laudato si'*, we can find some of these same values so important in Augustine: restlessness, relationships, respect:

> We are speaking of an attitude of the heart, one which approaches life with serene attentiveness, which is capable of being fully present to someone without thinking of what comes next, which accepts each moment as a gift from God to be lived to the full. Jesus taught us this attitude when he invited us to contemplate the lilies of the field and the birds of the air, or when seeing the rich young man and knowing his restlessness, "he looked at him with love" (Mk 10:21). He was completely present to everyone and to everything, and in this way, he showed us the way to overcome that unhealthy anxiety which makes us superficial, aggressive, and compulsive consumers.

The message of Augustine, as lived and taught by Fr. Art Purcaro, is something that will benefit the readers of this book. Just as Saint Augustine encourages the reader of his *Rule* to use it as if looking in a mirror, so too can this book be an opportunity for reflection and prayer, which can then become a new pathway to walk together with one another in harmony, in order to move forward in peace, with God and with the world around us.

Leo P.P. XIV

Preface

I am writing this while celebrating my fiftieth anniversary of priestly ordination. I chose to celebrate that day with a good friend of many years, from our time together in Peru and Rome, Cardinal Robert Prevost, O.S.A.

As it turns out, the day of my anniversary was the day of Pope Francis's funeral, so we both concelebrated, but not exactly as either one of us thought we would. Shortly after that, in God's wisdom, Cardinal Prevost became Pope Leo XIV, and I returned to my original plan, which was to spend time at our monastery in San Gimignano, Tuscany, to write the book that had been stirring in my heart for quite a while.

When Pope Leo stepped out on that balcony on May 8th, he let everyone know he is a son of Augustine, an Augustinian. As am I: born and raised in an Augustinian parish in the Bronx, New York; I entered the minor seminary at thirteen and the novitiate at seventeen, which was when the Chicago Province of the Order of Saint Augustine accepted Pope John XXIII's invitation to open a mission in Chulucanas, Peru. I volunteered.

I started in Peru in 1971 and knew from day one that this was what I was called to do. We had the chance to build the Church, which the Second Vatican Council had affirmed was needed, and the Bishops' Conference of Latin America spelled out for us, more in line with the Gospel Jesus announced in word and deed, inaugurating the reign of God. What a great privilege to be able to work with so many dedicated people: laity, religious, men and women, from many different backgrounds and countries, but most significantly, with the wonderful people of Chulucanas.

Preface

Those I met and worked with, friends eking out a subsistence-level existence in the Sechura Desert, along with families in the Andes Mountains, were isolated from one another by staggering distances and elevations to make their portion of communal land produce and keep their families alive.

Along with the people of Chulucanas, we lived through ten years of terrorist violence, which tried to stamp out any signs of progress in solidarity on behalf of the impoverished population. The terrorists wanted the huddled masses to rise up, throw out their government, and replace it with one more to their own ideological liking. They were openly against the colonial imperialism many nations endure even now.

Back in the United States, on home visits, is when it was hardest: to go into a store and see the abundance, the variety, the waste of which so many people were unaware. If God has created everything for everybody, why can't we do a better job of sharing with others, as God shares with us? There would be no violence, no hunger, no prejudice, if we could only recognize that we are one family, given one planet as our common home to share.

While dedicating my ministry to that goal, I was asked by my community to join the Augustinian leadership team in Rome to promote structural change more in line with these values. It was during this time in Rome, when Fr. Prevost became the Prior General of the Augustinian Order, that we had the chance to live and work together again for another six years.

I found expression for what was in my heart in Pope Francis's groundbreaking letter *On Care for Our Common Home* (*Laudato si'*). At sixty-five, I returned to my Augustinian Province in the United States and began to teach at Villanova University, where each semester I am surprised to find a class full of students interested in the two major topics I enjoy so much sharing with them: liberation theology and stewardship of creation.

My hope now is to be able to share with you what has been graciously shared with me: the wonderful gift from a loving God of so much bounty, which somehow we have managed to mangle and mess so that most of the people on our planet suffer want and misery to such a degree that it must bring God to tears.

This work is meant for anyone interested in living a more harmonious life. It is written for those who are not willing to accept the status quo, how things currently are, either for themselves, for others, or for nature itself. This is for those who want to be better, to do better, to share more. This is particularly for those women and men, young and old, laity and religious, who personally or in community, in their home or neighborhood, strive to follow *The Rule of Augustine* and want to continue to grow in the process of living in harmony.

The purpose is to encourage and assist in the process of caring for our common home and all its inhabitants, leaving no one out. *The Rule of Augustine* serves as a focus for greater attentiveness to the cry of the poor and of the planet founded on the interdependence and interrelationship of all of creation. It can be used in family or local community meetings, neighborhood or regional gatherings, as well as in programs of initial and ongoing formation.

General Introduction

Building a Better World: A Contemporary Augustinian Perspective is all about living in harmony. This is the fruit of my personal experience and that of many other Augustinian friars and laity striving to apply to our contemporary society the life promoted by Augustine in *The Rule* he wrote in Northern Africa over sixteen centuries ago.

A society and a world that places an exaggerated emphasis on a primarily individualistic spirituality and relationship with God, at the expense of relationships with others, ourselves, and the world around us, has yielded its fruit: external deserts that mirror our own interior desert, lamenting and reaching out restlessly to God.

Ours is an age of Trinitarian or communal spirituality that encourages us to demonstrate, by our deeds, that we have been created in the image and likeness of God-who-is-community. This is the right time for Augustinians to renew our commitment to community life and to communal holiness, giving witness in the Church and society in general to the particular gift of our charism, with one soul and one heart entirely centered on God.

The possibility of a more Christian culture or a civilization of love depends directly on the measure in which each one of us, our family, our community, and society itself, takes into account and bears witness to the fact that God wants to save and sanctify us, not individually and in isolation, but by forming a people (*Gaudium et Spes, Pastoral Constitution on the Church in the Modern World*, no. 9).

Harmony is defined as "a pleasing combination or arrangement of different things" or "a situation in which people are peaceful and agree with each other, or when things seem right or suitable together." In our world, we have too few experiences of true harmony, where differing positions and patterns achieve a balance through dialogue and compromise.

If we turn to current affairs, so much of what is in the news involves discord of some sort, conflicting concerns, escalating confrontations, and devastating violence. So much of our national history is a recounting of wars and battles; our heroes tend to be generals and other imposing figures. Tolerance and appreciation for diversity are fleeting virtues; harsh words and incompatibility serve to make the dream of living in harmony idyllic.

The biblical concept of harmony is a profound expression of God's desire for unity and peace among all people and all of creation. It calls us to reflect the intrinsic balance within the Trinity in our relationships and to work toward the restoration of God's intended plan for the world: abundant life for all, forever.

In a theological context, harmony is a vital aspect of Christian life, reflecting the unity and love that characterize the relationship between the Father, Son, and Holy Spirit. Through the practice of charity, humility, and forgiveness, believers are called to live in harmony and thereby glorify God and bear witness to God's transformative power in the world.

Yearning for harmony or communion has been at the heart of what it means to be human, a part of both our origin story and the goal of people, as well as of creation itself, throughout history. This restless search for harmony is in our DNA as well as in the destination point of our internal GPS—to become more fully alive to the extent that we go out of ourselves to enter into harmonious relationship, or communion, with God, self, others, and nature itself.

Pope Francis held up Saint Francis (for whom he took his name upon being chosen as pope) as an outstanding example of care for the vulnerable and nature itself, as a sign of an integral ecology lived out joyfully and authentically. The pope saw his namesake as principally concerned about God's creation and those who are impoverished and excluded, pointing to the saint's simple lifestyle and superb harmony with God, with others, with nature, and with himself (*Laudato si'*, no. 10).

Our understanding of God as Trinity, identified as harmonious relationship or communion, is what moves us to share as God shares with us: without condition and without limits. Jesus himself is the authentic witness to the call to give testimony to this truth, being a self for others, emptying his very self in order to share life in abundance with us and all of creation.

Harmony can be understood as becoming more attuned with the Creator, especially as conductor of creation. Similar to how a conductor leads an orchestra so that the music produced by the different instruments can be appreciated as a whole, so too the beauty of all creation can be appreciated because God, who is our Creator and conductor, not only assembles the elements of creation by calling all to come together but also created all to exist in balanced harmony.

The human-made dichotomy distinguishing the spiritual from the material serves to explain (or better, to excuse or attempt to justify) the constant but ever-growing abyss between the continually diminishing percentage who covet and collect constantly greater abundance, and the enormous majority of the human race that wallows in an ever diminishing share of what God has created for the good of all, and not just a few. It is as though possession of material goods, as some sort of exclusive or private property, was meant to be deserved or merited by a chosen few rather than shared and enjoyed among all as a gracious gift. Our restless longing for harmony calls us to live simply and share selflessly, so that all may simply live.

Harmony pursues appreciation for the spiritual and material dimensions of the unique reality of creation, which is called integral ecology.

Integral Ecology

Pope Francis's encyclical *Laudato si'*, subtitled *On Care for Our Common Home*, was a groundbreaking text that wove environmental concern into the fabric of Catholic theology. It introduced the concept of integral ecology, a view of the world where social, environmental, and economic issues are interdependent and need to be addressed together. The crisis we now face, given its complexity and interconnectedness, demands a new approach if we are to treat the roots of the crisis. This approach requires a new way of seeing, thinking, and acting, and offers a profound insight into how we can tackle the ecological crisis in an integrated way.

Integral ecology takes a holistic approach to human interaction with the environment, including the economic, social, political, cultural, ethical, and spiritual dimensions, highlighting the interconnectedness of all life on Earth. Such an ecology requires the vision and conviction to think about comprehensive solutions to both an environmental and a human crisis.

As Pope Francis astutely asserted in *Laudato si'* (no. 240), "the human person grows more, matures more and is sanctified more to the extent that he or she enters into relationships, going out from themselves to live in communion with God, with others and with all creatures." People centered on themselves fail to recognize a need for either God or others and readily treat them as objects while also considering the rest of creation to be in their power, subject to their domination.

Pope Francis declares that these four levels of relationships (self, God, others, and creation or the natural world) are interrelated and interdependent, making evident the need to be attentive to hear the cry of the poor and of the planet, to care for both creation and all our sisters and brothers, but with special concern for those who have been excluded from many of the benefits of God meant for all of us to share.

While the term integral ecology may be an unfamiliar one, the concept it embraces occupies an essential role in the Catholic Church's thinking and approach to tackling the environmental challenges today. Drawing upon the wealth of wisdom of the Church, Pope Francis urges us to view both the environmental and human crises through an integral approach, as a way for us all to work together to protect the Earth, our common home.

Integral ecology weaves together the myriad approaches to the natural world to respond as effectively and timely as possible to

General Introduction

the complex ecological problems that face us, our communities, and our world, in an evolving universe. In effect, integral ecology unites consciousness, culture, and nature in service of sustainability.

Faced with this global and urgent threat, many believe that we can engineer our way out of this crisis. After all, technology and the industrial revolution got us into this mess; therefore, the reasoning goes, technology and human ingenuity can get us out of it. But trying to solve the ecological crisis by developing new technical solutions can only treat the symptoms, not the cause.

When we view the crisis through the lens of integral ecology, rather than seeing each discrete problem in isolation, we begin to see that everything is deeply interconnected. This integrated view reveals a deeper insight. Not only are the ecological problems interconnected, but there is also an interconnection between the ecological crisis and the human crisis. For the human crisis, just like the environmental one, is made up of a wide range of issues affecting the human family; from extreme poverty to social inequality, from modern slavery to human trafficking, from poor working conditions to mass migration, and many more.

The insatiable desire for economic growth drives the production and market for ever-cheaper consumer goods, which drives the depletion of Earth's natural resources, and it is also a driver for cheap labor, which drives poor working conditions, which drives weak environmental standards, which drives pollution, which drives greenhouse emissions, which drives climate change, which destroys livelihoods, which drives mass migration, which drives growth in urbanization, which drives an increase in slum dwellings, which drives social inequality, which drives poor social and health services, which drives an increase in poverty, which drives despair and violence.

All of these issues are interconnected, and each problem cannot be solved without tackling the others. Integral ecology shows us that the ecological crisis is not simply a series of problems to be fixed but rather is a symptom of something that goes much deeper. Because at the heart of the ecological crisis lies a deep human and

General Introduction

spiritual crisis, in that we have forgotten who we are and where we have come from.

Nature is not something separate from us, or a mere setting in which we live, but rather we are part of nature, included in it and in constant interaction with it. Through the lens of integral ecology, we can see that we are faced not with two separate crises, one environmental and the other social, but rather with one complex crisis, which is both human and environmental. Or to put it another way, the cry of the earth and the cry of the poor are two sides of the same coin: creation. Everything is interconnected.

Just as ecology is the relationship of living organisms and their environment, we cannot regard ourselves as separate or disconnected from the ecosystems in which we live. Just as the Earth's ecosystems have worked harmoniously for millions of years, we too are part of a complex network of interconnected relationships that we may never fully comprehend or understand.

When we forget where we belong, we behave as lords and masters with dominion over creation, entitled to plunder her at will. Creation is viewed simply as an object to exploit. That same mindset of domination is also how we treat each other. When nature and humans are seen solely as a source of profit and gain, this has serious consequences for both our planet and the human family. This is why the human and ecological crises both share a common source.

When we view reality through the lens of integral ecology, we can see how all creation is a web of life that includes human and social dimensions. By understanding where we belong and our interconnectedness within the ecosystems that sustain us, we will no longer see God's creation as an object, there simply to serve our needs, but rather, we will come to a deeper understanding of our interdependence and our place of belonging within the delicate web of life.

By doing so, we can dedicate time and energy to care for each other, as well as the Earth, our common home. Given the urgency of our current situation, this new way of thinking and acting is needed now, more than ever. As a result, strategies for a solution demand an integrated approach to combating poverty, restoring dignity to the excluded, and, at the same time, protecting nature. In such an "economic ecology," the protection of the environment is seen as "an integral part of the development process and cannot be considered in isolation from it," as Pope Francis states.

The common good calls for respect for the human person as well as the overall welfare of society and the development of a variety of intermediate groups. It requires social peace, stability, and security, which cannot be achieved without particular concern for distributive justice (understood as a fair distribution, equitable allocation, or just apportionment of resources and benefits within a society). For Pope Francis, it is obvious that "where injustices abound and growing numbers of people are deprived of basic human rights and considered expendable, the principle of the common good immediately becomes, logically and inevitably, a summons to solidarity and a preferential option for the poorest of our brothers and sisters."

Saint Augustine

Augustine (named pretentiously a "little emperor" after the Roman Emperor Augustus) was born in Tagaste, in Northern Africa, in AD 354. Monica, his mother, was a Christian of indigenous Berber ethnicity, and Patricius, his father, a mid-level Roman official, identified with the Roman Empire, which ruled this part of the world and treated it as its breadbasket. The culture in which they lived was Roman. These loving parents craved and planned for their child to be successful in the Roman fashion: to have a profession and command respect, so as to provide for them in their old age.

After a typical Roman education, their son certainly achieved their dream: He became an orator or rhetorician of the Roman Emperor, in Milan, well remunerated, surrounded by fawning family and fans. At the very height of his career, he turned his back on the prestigious position, along with the fame and salary accompanying what he had achieved, to follow Christ by living the radical communion of goods exemplified in the Acts of the Apostles. He, and those closest to him, converted and were baptized in the Catholic faith.

General Introduction

Augustine and his entourage returned to his birthplace, Tagaste, to the humble piece of property his father had left him, and gathered those who wanted a life in common, where all things were shared among the community members while generously taking care of the neighboring poor, after the example of Christ and his disciples. This path was chosen by those who wished to serve God and others by sharing material and spiritual goods with them, to better bear witness to the God they served, a God who they understood to be dynamic relationship, unbounded goodness, who in Christ emptied himself to become not only one with us but our servant.

Augustine was enamored of the ideal presented in the Acts of the Apostles, describing life in the primordial Christian community of Jerusalem in which the believers shared their possessions:

> They devoted themselves to the apostles' teaching and to fellowship, to the breaking of bread, and to prayer. Everyone was filled with awe at the many wonders and signs performed by the apostles. All the believers were together and had everything in common. They sold property and possessions to give to anyone who had need. Every day, they continued to meet together in the temple courts. They broke bread in their homes and ate together with glad and sincere hearts, praising God and enjoying the favor of all the people. And the Lord added to their number daily those who were being saved. (Acts 2:42-47)

> All the believers were one in heart and mind. No one claimed that any of their possessions was their own, but they shared everything they had. With great power, the apostles continued to testify to the resurrection of the Lord Jesus. And God's grace was so powerfully at work in them all that there were no needy persons among them. For from time to time, those who owned land or houses sold them, brought the money from the sales and put it at the apostles' feet, and it was distributed to anyone who had need. (Acts 4:32-35)

General Introduction

Harmony, as Augustine understood it, was not a permanent state but an ongoing process that required careful attention, attentive listening, and sustained practice through dialogue. Augustine experienced the disruptive decline of the Roman Empire, as internal struggles and invasions drove the vast realm toward collapse. In this atmosphere, Augustine centered much attention on peace, not simply as the absence of violence, but as a harmonious relationship of justice and friendship. In Book XIV of his opus, *The City of God*, Augustine wrote: "God desired not only that the human race might be able by their similarity of nature to associate with one another, but also that they might be bound together in harmony and peace by the ties of relationship."

Augustine's early community in Tagaste developed into a movement when Augustine was chosen, in the fashion of the times, to become priest, then bishop, of the Catholic Christian community in nearby Hippo, an African port city, which would later be conquered by invading Vandals shortly after Augustine died in AD 430.

Augustine was able to establish a community to join him as a priest, and another community when he was made bishop. Many people followed the example of their pastor and established similar communities in the surrounding countryside.

It is believed that, to provide basic guidelines for these early communities, around the year 397, Augustine penned, in outline form, an appropriate orientation, which was gathered and copied repeatedly, in order to be shared. The original document is known to us as *The Rule of Augustine*, and it guides many groups of men and women religious, as well as the laity, throughout the world today. It allows us to benefit from Augustine's comprehension of the importance of self-awareness and awareness of the presence of God.

As is frequently the case in the Fathers of the Church, Augustine refers in a masterly way to the allegorical interpretation of the Scriptures. In Augustine, we find a series of rich and expressive texts that illustrate the ideal of living in harmony through the images of the building of the temple and musical harmony.

General Introduction

The Choir

What is a symphony? The harmony of voices ... It is the symphony to which the Apostle referred when he said: I urge you brothers, all to speak the same thing, that there be no divisions between you (1 Cor 1:10). Who does not delight in this holy symphony, that is to say, the harmony of voices, not each one going its own way, without anything inadequate or out of tune, that might offend the ear of an expert? Harmony is of the essence of the choir. In a choir, what is pleasing is the single voice, as a result of many others, which maintains unity without dissonance or discordant notes. (Sermon 119A, 9)

Praise his name in choir. What is a choir? Many of you know what it is and, precisely since I am speaking in the city, without doubt, almost all of you know. A choir is a group of singers who sing with one voice. If we sing in choir, let us sing harmoniously. Any discrepancy of voice in the choir of singers offends the ear and disturbs the choir. If the voice of the singer is out of tune and disturbs the harmonious canticle, how much more will dissonant heresy disturb the harmony of those giving praise? The whole world already forms the choir of Christ. Christ's choir resounds from East to West. Then another Psalm says: From the time the sun rises until it sets, praise the name of the Lord. Praise his name in choir. With kettledrum and psaltery let them give praise. Why take up the kettledrum and the psaltery? So that not only the voice praises, but also your acts. When the psaltery and the kettledrum are taken up, the hands accompany the voice. This will happen to you if, when you sing the hallelujah, you are offering bread to the hungry, you are clothing the naked and welcoming the pilgrim, since then not only is the voice singing, but the hands are accompanying it, since works go hand in hand with voices. You picked up the musical instrument, may your hands accompany your tongue. Nor must the ministry be encompassed by the psaltery and the kettledrum fall silent either. (Sermon 149, 7-8)

You are the trumpet, the psaltery, the zither, the drum, the choir, the strings, the organ, and the sounding cymbal of merriment in the things that sound good, because they are harmonious. Do not think here of anything mean or superficial or vulgar. And, since perceiving according to the flesh is death, let every spirit praise the Lord! (Sermon 150, 8)

The Temple

What happened here, when this building was raised, happens now when the faithful in Christ come together. Believing is, in a certain sense, equivalent to drawing the trees and stones from the woods and mountains; being catechized and formed is comparable to the task of felling, polishing, and smoothing in the hands of the carpenters and stonemasons. Nevertheless, these beams and stones do not set up the house of God more than when one or the other of them are adjusted through charity. If these beams and these stones are not combined in a certain order, if they are not peacefully adjusted, if in any way they are not brought together in a mutual embrace, no one would enter here. (Sermon 336, 1)

Place the counsels of the prophets and the apostles as cement in your hearts. Lay your humility in front of you, as a smooth and flat pavement. Defend together, in your hearts, the salutary doctrine with prayer and the Word, as firm walls. Light them up with the divine witnesses as if they were lamps. Support the weak as if you were columns. Shelter the needy under the roofs, that the Lord our God may recompense the worldly goods with eternal goods and may possess you forever once the building is completed, built and dedicated. (Sermon 337, 5)

General Introduction

The Augustinian Order

In the Middle Ages (1244), the Church called into existence the Augustinian Order, uniting under Augustine's *Rule*, or *Way of Life*, small communities of hermits in Tuscany, and later (1256) convoking other hermit groups, to promote the evangelical vision of the essential equality of all Christians (all were called "brothers" rather than "Lords"), dressing simply and sharing their material and spiritual goods. Their government was decentralized and reflected the active participation of all, as well as the understanding of authority as service to the community. The "superior" was to be called "prior" since his role was to be first among brothers, a builder and facilitator of community life. Their houses, just as in Augustine's time some eight centuries earlier, would have a chapel to recognize the importance of common prayer—since Augustine believed we cannot build the reign of harmony and peace without God—but also a library, recognizing and encouraging the value of studies for furthering the cause of that reign.

This lifestyle proved attractive, and the Order of Saint Augustine grew. Within a century of its founding, there were more than eight thousand friars who professed and lived this way of life in many parts of Europe. Women religious were also aggregated to the Augustinian Order, and many lay women and men shared Augustinian spirituality and liturgical customs as members of Augustinian lay fraternities.

Today, there are close to three thousand Augustinian friars around the world, gathered in forty-five provinces or administrative units, present in more than fifty countries. Around 1,500 Augustinian contemplative nuns are members of the Order of Saint Augustine. There are also communities of Augustinian sisters who work in ministry outside of their convent. To these are added many members of groups of lay Augustinians as well as numerous lay faithful affiliated with the Order.

The very reason for our coming together as Augustinians has always been to encourage one another to live together in harmony, striving to follow the way of life revealed by Christ, to share as

God shares with us: freely and generously. We know we need one another to do this, and that the more we go out of ourselves to relate to one another, to creation itself, to God, and to our very own self, the more fully alive, the more fully human, the more like God we can become. We know we cannot do it alone: We need God, and the glory of God is humanity fully alive, as Saint Irenaeus stated over eighteen centuries ago. The more we share, the more truly like Christ we become.

The world today, specifically our materialistic, consumer-oriented culture, is permeated by individualism (selfishness, greed, hunger for power and pleasure). This points directly to the need for a more faithful witness to an alternative to that generally accepted lifestyle in which we find ourselves immersed. This is the meaning of our way of life, our purpose for existence, our hope for the world: to give credible witness to the value of relationships, of living in harmony with one another, while respecting and celebrating diversity. We believe we are called to model and promote this lifestyle in all we say and do.

The Rule of Augustine continues to call us to evangelical sharing, attentive to the cry of the poor as well as to that of the planet, since everything is interrelated and interconnected, through an integral ecology. In fidelity to the gospel principles and *The Rule of Augustine*, we are called to be socially critical.

Through our expressed intention to follow Christ in the footsteps of Augustine, we strive to give witness to, and work for, the building up of a better world for all, not just for some. For followers of Christ, the building up of community is an ongoing process of forging and fortifying ever-expanding concentric circles, sharing gifts and talents, attending to needs and wants, always reaching out, especially to those most in need, never closing the door, and never excluding. Communion, as manifested by the harmonious diversity of the Trinity, is our model and goal. Dialogue is the path toward that goal, and we, working together as a community, are called to be instruments of communion, witnesses to the joy that following Christ entails. We all have something to offer; we all need one another. We are better together.

General Introduction

Reaching out, seeking ever-new pathways to draw people in, to share all God's gifts with everybody, as God planned from the beginning, is essential to our mission as followers of Christ in the Augustinian way of life. We search together for truth, sharing the journey, sharing the fruits.

Communal Holiness: Living in Harmony

A community is much more than the sum of its parts; in fact, a healthy, healing, holy community is a catalyst for growth precisely due to its harmonious nature. In that sense, a community is similar to a mosaic: Take just one piece out and the whole design is affected. Harmony can be messy and requires constant intentional effort.

The concept of living in harmony is very much in tune with Augustine's thought, particularly in what refers to religious life. Augustine, after being ordained a priest, introduced this communal lifestyle as a clear alternative to the particularly selfish society of the time.

Augustine constantly emphasized fraternal love as an expression of the communion that flows from our sharing in the divine life. Fraternity, for Augustine, is a form of true worship and is conducive to harmonious living. The biblical concept of koinonia or sharing is the basis for his spirituality and ecclesiology. The sharing of material and spiritual goods is the soul of Augustinian religious life; what we truly share is not so much material possessions as God, our one true treasure.

Community life, for Augustine, means transcendence, tending toward what is holy, dynamic, and life-giving, and doing this not just in community but also as a community, encouraging one another along the way. To truly share God, we must share also our material goods, which requires of us profound interpersonal relations based on love. For Augustine, the ascent toward God requires the support of the community.

Community is never to be understood as uniformity, in the Augustinian model. Nine times in his brief *Rule*, Augustine indicates the importance of respecting the uniqueness of each member, recognizing their own particular needs. Living in harmony does not repress each member's identity but rather promotes and encourages respect for diversity and growth in the particular gifts each one has received in service to the community; hence, harmonious living.

"All should live united in mind and heart and should in one another honor God whose temples you have become" (*Rule*, chapter 1, par. 8). Augustinians, united in love, make manifest and give witness to the presence of God among us, in our world. In this way, communal holiness contributes to the transformation of our society, which is ever more individualistic and utilitarian.

Christ has promised to be with those who gather in his name. This combines with the impossibility of one single person or even one community to contain the fullness of the holiness of God. It becomes natural for us, then, to speak of harmony or communal holiness, as a gift from God to cherish and foster, as well as to celebrate as a constitutive element in the identity and ideal of our Order, including those generations who have gone before us and are now considered to be among the communion of saints of the Augustinian family. Their joint witness to the communal nature of holiness must be kept alive in our memory to spur us on as well.

Augustine and the Environment

Augustine's teaching on love of neighbor is understood as directly relevant to love of nature. The effect can be profound and provocative. We are encouraged to comprehend that when we love nature in the right way (not in a sense of exclusive possessiveness or for dominion or self-aggrandizement), we are participating in the very nature of God because God is love. We are brought to grasp that love of God and love of nature cannot be separated.

Sincere love moves us to seek the happiness of all creatures, expecting no other advantage than their happiness. Indeed, the most concrete way to love God would be to love the poor and the suffering creatures with whom God identifies in a particular fashion.

Augustine had a radical change of heart inspired by his ever-growing belief and relationship with Jesus Christ as the Son of

God. Augustine is often admired for his conversion experience, not a once-and-done activity but rather an ongoing process, from the womb that bore him to the tomb that received him seventy-six years later. Augustine, a spiritual master in his own right, was more accurately a follower, a true disciple of Christ, a member of the community of people who knew themselves to be chosen, called to join together with others to follow Christ.

What does Augustine have to say to us about our environment? The foundation of it all is Christ. Augustinian God-talk is centered on and emanates from Augustine's relationship with Christ.

To be an Augustinian means to follow Christ in an Augustinian fashion: in a personal, ongoing relationship and process of conversion. That is to say, always "on the way", never fully arrived, walking in the footsteps of Augustine, informed and enhanced by his personal (and communal) experience. That ongoing relationship and conversion process is what can speak to us across the centuries to help us better understand how a follower of Christ can interpret the world in which we live, or specifically, in this case, our environment. We follow Christ, not Augustine, and to the extent that Augustine's experience enlightens us on that path, we are Augustinians, following Christ in an Augustinian fashion.

Some of Augustine's most famous works, admired by many throughout the ages, are *On the Trinity*, *The City of God*, and the *Confessions*. We could certainly find much enlightenment concerning Augustine's understanding of the issue of the environment in each of those major works. However, for this reflection, we center our attention on a much more concise and truly popular document—in that it has been read avidly and followed by many more people over the centuries—which Augustine wrote at the age of forty-three, some ten years after his own baptism: his *Rule of Life*. Written to foster and facilitate for his contemporaries the path walked by the early Christian community (Acts 2:32-37, 4:42-47), Augustine gathered in a diminutive document—consisting of only eight brief chapters—some basic principles, easily applied and adapted by those who would choose to take them on as a way of living, be they families in their home, nuns gathered in their convent, monks in their monastery, or clergy in what we now call a rectory.

I encourage you to study *The Rule of Augustine*, not out of mere curiosity, nor to discover the foibles and peculiarities of how people lived over sixteen centuries ago at the time of the decline and fall of the Roman Empire, particularly in its colony in Northern Africa, but rather to consider how Augustine's presentation of some basic Christian principles might lead you and me and all of us, to a better life: enough for all, forever (a concise way of defining the concept of sustainability).

The first essential principle emphasized by Augustine regarding the topic of sustainability is dignity—the innate worth of each and every human being. Each person, the whole person, and all people. We are all of infinite worth. Augustine states clearly in chapter 1 of the *Rule*: "Honor God in one another whose temples you have become."

Human dignity is the foundational principle of all Catholic social teaching and is based on the firm belief that we are all created in the image and likeness of God. Human dignity is inalienable, an essential and intrinsic quality of every human being, not derived from legal mandate or individual merit or accomplishment.

Discover God, honor God, in ourselves, in one another, aware that no one is worth more, no one worth less. We are each and all of infinite worth that does not depend on the color of our skin or our economic status. Our worth resides not in our possessions, in what we have, but rather in who we are: the image and likeness of our divine Creator. Truly, as Augustine states in one of his most celebrated phrases: "You have made us for yourself, Lord, and our hearts are restless until they rest in you" (*Confessions* I, i) We are invited as well as destined to become more sanctified, more like God, more relational, as the Trinity itself is. The more we relate, the more truly human we become.

Remember, Augustine is writing in the land of his birth, in Northern Africa, and his audience is men and women of various racial backgrounds, as well as diverse social and economic statuses. There were affluent landowners as well as those of a more humble, rural background, indigenous people, the Berbers (like Augustine's mother, Monica); there were those who aspired to be accepted in the rapidly declining but actively imposing social network of the Roman Empire (like Augustine's own father, Patricius). They were all invited to find God in themselves and one another, excluding no one. In Augustine's own community in Hippo, the previously wealthy learned to live in harmony with former slaves. No one was entitled to take sole ownership of what God had gifted to all people. The more we share, the more truly Christian—Christ-like—we become.

A basic principle underlying Augustine's spirituality and encouraging social responsibility is that God created all that exists for everyone:

> Do you think it's a small matter that you are eating someone else's food? Listen to the apostle: We brought nothing into this world. You have come into the world, you have found a full table spread for you. But the Lord's is the earth and its fullness. God bestows the world on the poor, he bestows it on the rich. (Sermon 29, 2)

> The possession of goodness is by no means diminished by being shared with a partner either permanent or temporarily assumed; on the contrary, the possession of goodness is increased in proportion to the concord and charity of each of those who share it. (*The City of God*, XV, 5)

Tarsicius van Bavel, an Augustinian scholar of the twentieth century, wrote in his Introduction to *The Rule*:

> We could characterize the Rule of Augustine as a call to the evangelical equality of all people. It voices the Christian demand to bring all men and women into full communion. At the same time, it sounds an implicit protest against inequality in a society which is so clearly marked by possessiveness, pride, and power. According to Augustine, a monastic community should offer an alternative by striving to build a community that is

General Introduction

not motivated by possessiveness, pride, and power, but by love for one another. And, in this sense, the Rule of Augustine is also socially critical.

The Augustinian theme of communion as well as the Pauline notion of the "body of Christ" echo the reality of a web of relationships that sustain life in all its forms on the planet, our common home. The circle of communion is enlarged to encompass all of creation and not just human beings alone. While the essential principle of Catholic social thought, the dignity of every human being, is recognized and validated, the intrinsic value of everything God created is identified uniquely and validated in their mutual relationship with one another.

Augustine interprets the notion of the body of Christ in terms of the *totus Christus*, the whole Christ, which is meant to include all those inhabitants across the entire planet, as well as our common home itself, with a view toward when Christ will be all in all.

Pope Francis calls the common good a second principle of Catholic social thought, "a central and unifying principle of social ethics." Quoting *Gaudium et Spes,* the Second Vatican Council's *Pastoral Constitution on the Church in the Modern World*, he defines the common good as "the sum of those conditions of social life which allow social groups and their individual members relatively thorough and ready access to their own fulfillment." The notion of the common good calls into question the accumulation of material goods.

Augustine clarifies in Chapter 5 of *The Rule*: "the more you are concerned about the common good rather than your own, the more progress you will know that you have made." Caring for and about what we hold in common is our vocation.

Creation itself is our common good, the Earth our common home, a gift of God to us, to all of us, that takes into account future generations as well, but not merely for us, but for us to share. All of God's good gifts are given to all of us, and not to be enjoyed fully by simply a few of us, but have been given to us to share, just as God has shared these gifts with us. This is the Augustinian golden rule regarding a truly sustainable life for all, a veritable ecology based on justice, understood as right relationships, on all four levels: how we relate to ourselves, to our Creator, to one another, and to the rest of creation as well.

Far from any pantheistic interpretation, Augustine declares clearly how we can discover something of God in nature, but God is not identified with nature:

> This is what I love when I love my God. And what is this? I put my question to the earth and it replied 'I am not he'; I questioned everything it held, and they confessed the same. I questioned the sea and the great deep, and the teeming live creatures that crawl, and they replied, 'We are not God; seek higher.' I questioned the gusty winds, and every breeze with all its flying creatures told me, 'Anaximenes was wrong: I am not God'. To the sky I put my question, to sun, moon, stars, but they denied me: 'We are not the God you seek. And to all things which stood around the portals of my flesh I said: Tell me of my God. You are not he, but tell me something of him.' Then they lifted up their voices and cried: 'He made us.' My questioning was my attentive spirit, and their reply, their beauty. (*Confessions*, X, vi)

Pope Francis's vision of integral ecology and the common good includes justice between generations. Returning to his biblical vision, he says that "the world is a gift we have freely received and must share with others." This includes future generations. "The world we have received also belongs to those who will follow us." He asks: "What kind of world do we want to leave to those who will come after us, to children who are now growing up?"

The third principle evident in Augustine's *Rule of Life* is subsidiarity: the belief that everyone has something to offer and that all are responsible for being agents of our own destiny. Augustine's exposition on authority and service, understood as followers of Christ, stood in stark contrast to the predominantly Roman practice accepted at the time Augustine was writing. We find a marked difference in the call to participation, the need to adapt according to diverse needs and possibilities, which Augustine expounds, and the society in which he (and we) finds himself. Subsidiarity emphasizes the need for consultation and participation, for doing *with* those affected rather than doing *for* them, inspiring each one to assume personal responsibility for the building up of a better world for all, rather than fostering a sense of dependence and paternalism. Everything is interconnected, interrelated, and interdependent. From these flows the appreciation for and promotion of mutuality, partnership, cooperation, reciprocity, and sharing—all expressions of the principle of subsidiarity—which emanates from respect for the dignity of every human being. Subsidiarity means "to help" or "assist," indicating that senior levels have an obligation to help individuals and subordinate groups to flourish, while avoiding the danger of swamping or absorbing them. Those most affected by decisions need to have a place at the table when decisions are made, based on the firm belief that we each have something to offer. We all have something to offer; no one is worth more or less, and consequently, each and every one needs to be taken into account, not treated as an object.

The fourth and final principle, solidarity, is testified to amply in *The Rule* as well as in many of the other writings of Augustine, which have survived and come to us across sixteen centuries of existence in a turbulent world. And so, for Augustine, as for Christ and so too for Christians, reaching out in solidarity to help the poor is a matter of justice, not merely charity:

> Christ who is rich in heaven chose to be hungry in the poor. Yet in your humanity you hesitate to give to your fellow human being. Don't you realize that what you give, you give to Christ, from whom you received whatever you have to give in the first place? (*Commentary on Psalm* 75:9)
>
> You give bread to a hungry person; but it would be better were no one hungry, and you could give it to no one. You clothe the naked person. Would that all were clothed and this necessity did not exist. (*Tractate* 1 John 8:8)

General Introduction

Beyond wishing well, we are called to do good, to share, to try to level the playing field a bit more so that we can all benefit from the goods of creation for which God determined a universal destination. Augustine's *Rule* provides a concrete expression of this basic Christian principle founded on the firm belief in the inherent and enduring dignity of each and every human being.

For this to become more of a reality, the principle of solidarity needs to be exercised. Solidarity is action motivated by love, inspired by concern for the well-being of all. Solidarity implies that those who have more are called to share more. Solidarity is a firm and persevering determination to commit to the good of each person and all.

The principles expounded in Augustine's *Rule* are meant to encourage and guide social action on behalf of a better world in which we can demonstrate that there is truly enough for all, forever.

Love Is the Essential Nucleus

Opening Exhortation of *The Rule of Augustine*

1. We urge you who form a religious community to put the following precepts into practice.
2. Before all else, brothers, we must love God and our neighbor because these are the greatest commandments.

―·····―

We take heart from the guidance Pope Francis has provided in *Laudato si'* (*On Care for Our Common Home*) in identifying the root of our problem:

> Men and women of our postmodern world run the risk of rampant individualism, and many problems of society are connected with today's self-centered culture of instant gratification. (no. 162)

> Disinterested concern for others, and the rejection of every form of self-centeredness and self-absorption, are essential if we truly wish to care for our brothers and sisters and for the natural environment. These attitudes also attune us to the moral imperative of assessing the impact of our every action and personal decision on the world around us. If we can overcome individualism, we will truly be able to develop a different lifestyle and bring about significant changes in society. (no. 208)

Sin interrupts God's plan for creation; individualism, or selfishness, disrupts the harmony that God intended to reign among us. Breaking the bond of harmony, of communion with God, causes a rupture in the internal unity of the human person, in the relations of harmony between woman and man, and in the harmonious relations between humankind and other creatures and with nature itself.

It is reasonable that contemporary commentary on *The Rule of Augustine* places a certain emphasis on the relationship we have with nature, God's creative gift to us to share. We interpret the Gospel mandate to love God and our neighbor in the sense that Pope Francis has emphasized: the interdependence and interrelationship between the cry of the poor and that of the planet itself. These spheres are not independent or indifferent to one another; however, they critically interact, so that when we ignore the plight of the impoverished or excluded person, we are also disregarding the consequences for the natural world, and vice versa.

An imbalance in care for the marginalized has direct consequences for the environment, be it the geographical area in which they are redlined, or the contaminated air they are destined to breathe.

What good does it do to provide education for a healthy diet to people saddled by grossly inadequate salaries, corralled into neighborhoods without access to fresh groceries or the most elemental health care, with drinking water from insufficiently protected sources and deteriorating plumbing? If Flint, Michigan, or Grays Ferry, Pennsylvania, come to mind, you get the picture.

To love God and our neighbor, we must also love and care for the environment in which we live. Augustine's *Rule* reminds us that life in abundance is everyone's destiny, and those who choose to follow Christ in the footsteps of Augustine are invited to contribute to building a better world for all, not one in which some feel compelled to live behind closed walls or gated communities, which ultimately isolate and foster division rather than communion and wholeness.

Personal sin has social consequences, and the accumulation of those consequences systematically infiltrates our social structures. It is in the breakdown of our relationships, spurred on by our selfishness and radical individualism, that we find the deepest roots of all the evils that afflict social relations between people and all situations in economic and political life that attack the dignity of the person, that assail justice and solidarity, while radically affecting our planet as well.

And yet, life in abundance is generously shared with us in Jesus by God the Father's initiative and brought about and transmitted by the work of the Holy Spirit. Universal and integral salvation for all people and for the whole person is offered. This concerns the human person in all our dimensions—personal and social, spiritual and corporeal, historical and transcendent—making indissoluble the link between the relationship that the person is called to have with God and the responsibility we have toward our neighbor in the concrete circumstances of history and with the created universe.

We are reminded by the *Pastoral Constitution of the Church in the Modern World* promulgated by the Second Vatican Council, (paraphrased for inclusivity):

> Redeemed by Christ and made a new creature in the Holy Spirit, humanity can, indeed must, love the things of God's creation: it is from God that we have received them, and it is as flowing from God's hand that we look upon them and revere them. Humanity thanks our divine benefactor for all these things, using them and enjoying them in a spirit of poverty and freedom. Thus, we are brought to a true possession of the world, as having nothing yet possessing everything: "All [things] are yours; and you are Christ's; and Christ is God's." (1 Cor 3:22-23)[37]

Augustine identified a specific way of living the Christian message, not the only way, but as a gift or charism that allows us to perceive the whole from a particular viewpoint. That gift emphasizes the social or communal nature of our very being, to which all are called. Pope Francis reminded us of this calling (as many popes and holy women and men throughout the centuries have done) when he wrote:

> The Father is the ultimate source of everything, the loving and self-communicating foundation of all that exists. The Son, his reflection, through whom all things were created, united himself to this earth when he was formed in the womb of Mary. The Spirit, infinite bond of love, is intimately present at the very heart of the universe, inspiring and bringing new pathways. (*Laudato si'*, no. 238)
>
> The human person grows more, matures more, and is sanctified more, to the extent that he or she enters into relationships going out from themselves, to live in communion with God, with others, and with all creatures.
>
> In this way, they make their own that trinitarian dynamism which God imprinted in them when they were created. Everything is interconnected, and this invites us to develop a spirituality of that global solidarity which flows from the mystery of the Trinity. (*Laudato si'*, no. 240)

An important dimension of Augustine's lifelong conversion is his conviction that human beings can reveal to one another the goodness of God, growing together in harmony. We do this personally, communally, and institutionally. This is not an individual effort, but a personal one: We are called to share generously, as God shares with us.

To be an Augustinian means to follow Christ in an Augustinian fashion: in a personal, ongoing relationship and process of conversion. That is to say, always on the way, never fully arrived, walking in the footsteps of Augustine, informed and enhanced by his personal (and communal) experience. That ongoing relationship and conversion process is what can speak to us across the centuries to help us better understand how a follower of Christ can interpret the world in which we live, or specifically, in this case, our environment. We follow Christ, not Augustine, and to the extent that Augustine's experience enlightens us on that path, we are Augustinians, following Christ in an Augustinian fashion.

Once again, we turn to Pope Francis's tome *On Care of our Common Home* to remind us:

> Our relationship with the environment can never be isolated from our relationship with others and with God. Otherwise, it would be nothing more than romantic individualism dressed up in ecological garb, locking us into a stifling immanence. (no. 119)

> Neglecting to monitor the harm done to nature and the environmental impact of our decisions is only the most striking sign of a disregard for the message contained in the structures of nature itself. When we fail to acknowledge as part of reality the worth of a poor person, a human embryo, a person with disabilities—to offer just a few examples—it becomes difficult to hear the cry of nature itself; everything is connected. (no. 117)

> There can be no renewal of our relationship with nature without a renewal of humanity itself. (no. 118))

This Opening Exhortation of Augustine's *Rule* starkly states that loving relationships in harmony are the goal, the essential nucleus of all creation, and the specific precept, or task, of those committed to follow Christ in the footsteps of Augustine include loving God and loving our neighbor by also caring for the habitat in which these harmonious relationships are meant to flourish.

We recall Pope Francis's admonition in *On Care for Our Common Home*:

> Disregard for the duty to cultivate and maintain a proper relationship with my neighbor, for whose care and custody I am responsible, ruins my relationship with my own self, with others, with God and with the earth. When all these relationships are neglected, when justice no longer dwells in the land, the Bible tells us that life itself is endangered. (no. 70)

The Ideal Toward Which We Strive: Harmony

Setting the Scene: A Christmas Vignette

To reflect on our ideal, we take as a point of departure our reality, striving to keep our eyes on the prize: living in harmony.

We recall the past, not to wallow in nostalgia, pining for how things used to be, but rather to rededicate ourselves to a better future, more aligned and in tune with our ideals and values.

The Purcaro family lived in the Bronx in the 1950s: four children under ten years of age. Dad was a New York City policeman; Mom worked part-time as a school crossing guard. Income was not abundant but loving care certainly was. Come Christmas, our eyes lit up as the Christmas tree was purchased and decorated on Christmas Eve. After going to Mass as a family, and pancakes with lots of syrup, we were led with great anticipation to the tree to discover our gifts. There were two or three for each one of us, depending on that year's financial situation. We each took our turn opening one, admiring what the others got, until all was done.

All four of us will always remember the first time we heard those words from our father: "Okay kids, time to pick one of your gifts." Sounded strange but we didn't have much time to think about it because it was soon followed by the instruction: Now go get your coats. Our coats! What for? And Dad's response went right to the heart and has rested there since, burrowing ever deeper, from quandary to different levels of comprehension: "We're going to the orphanage. There are lots of kids there like you but who don't have anyone to give them a gift this Christmas. You have several gifts and just as they were shared with you, so now you have the chance to share them with someone else."

Lesson learned: Everything is gift, freely given. Gifts are for sharing, not stashing. Share the joy, the knowledge that someone cares enough to share.

The Rule of Augustine, Chapter 1

3. Before all else, live together in harmony, being of one mind and one heart on the way to God. For is it not precisely for this reason that you have come to live together?

4. Among you, there can be no question of personal property. Rather, take care that you share everything in common. Your superior should see to it that each person is provided with food and clothing. He does not have to give exactly the same to everyone, for you are not all equally strong, but each person should be given what he personally needs. For this is what you read in the Acts of the Apostles: "Everything they owned was held in common, and each one received whatever he had need of" (4:32, 35).

5. Those who owned possessions in the world should readily agree that, from the moment they enter religious life, these become the property of the community.

6. Those who did not have possessions ought not to strive in the religious community for what they could not obtain outside of it. One must have, indeed, regard for their frailty by providing for them whatever they need, even if they were formerly so poor that they could not even afford the necessities of life. They may not, however, consider themselves fortunate because they now receive food and clothing, which were beyond their means in earlier years.

7. Nor should they give themselves airs because they now find themselves in the company of people whom they would not have ventured to approach before. Their heart should seek for nobler things, not vain earthly appearance. If, in their religious life, rich people were to become humble and the poor people haughty, then this style of life would seem to be of value only to the rich and not to the poor.

8. On the other hand, let those who appear to have had some standing in the world not look down upon their brothers who have entered the religious community from a condition of poverty. They ought to be more mindful of their life together with poor brothers than of the social status of their wealthy parents. And the fact that they have made some of their possessions available to the community gives them no reason to have a high opinion of themselves. Otherwise, people would more easily fall prey to pride in sharing riches with the community than they would have done if they had enjoyed them in the world. For while all vices manifest themselves in wrongdoing, pride lurks also in our good works, seeking to destroy even them. What good does it do to distribute one's possessions to the poor and to become poor oneself, if giving up riches makes the person prouder than he was when he had a fortune?

9. You are all to live together, therefore, "one in mind and one in heart," and honor God in one another because "each of you has become his temple."

The Ideal Toward Which We Strive: Harmony

The first chapter of *The Rule* contains what Augustine considered the most significant fundamentals for following Christ:

- Recognize that everything is gift;
- Realize that gifts are meant to be enjoyed and shared, as God shares with us: generously, without conditions or limits;
- Steep ourselves in humility, a two-sided coin, to understand that we all have something to offer or share; and that we all need others to share their gifts with us;
- Have gratitude to God who inspires the good work in us and gives us the strength to follow through: We honor God in one another.

Living in harmony is sharing communion, the great gift of God-self; our one, true, common inheritance is God. Pope Francis stated clearly in *On Care for Our Common Home*:

> Whether believers or not, we are agreed today that the earth is essentially a shared inheritance, whose fruits are meant to benefit everyone. For believers, this becomes a question of fidelity to the Creator, since God created the world for everyone. Hence every ecological approach needs to incorporate a social perspective which takes into account the fundamental rights of the poor and the underprivileged. (no. 93)

As a starting point, Augustine recognized that material poverty is not God's will for us, nor the result of fate or passivity; poverty is not caused by God to punish us but rather by us, through our rupturing of God's harmonious plan for communion—abundant life for all.

What Is Meant by Material Poverty?

To be poor is to be weak, indigent, wretched, and at the mercy of others. To be poor means to be listless, inattentive, to die—slowly—of hunger, to be illiterate, to have no access to basic health care, to not recognize that you are a person with innate dignity and invaluable worth.

The poor are victims, vulnerable and dependent, the result of a sundering of human solidarity and communion with God. The poor have no voice, their opinion does not count; they are left out, shamed, considered worth less than others. Material poverty, then, is a subhuman, scandalous situation, not the result of either fate or laziness. Material poverty means not having the basic conditions for a truly human life. Poverty is inimical to human dignity. Material poverty is degrading and contrary to the will of God.

Material poverty is not good, not the will of God. At whose feet shall we lay it? Free will allows us to be selfish, to thwart God's plan for abundant life for all. Selfishness, stinginess, and indifference in the face of suffering are among the major causes of material poverty.

As such, material poverty is a manifestation of sinfulness, selfishness, and prioritizing myself and my needs over those of others. Material poverty sparks an imbalance, a rupture of harmony, a fracturing of communion, discord, incoherence, disagreement, disorder, confusion, turmoil, disarray, dissonance, and dissension.

The word "poverty" is inadequate and does not truly reflect the reality: "Impoverished" expresses better the truth that underlies the experience of hunger and want. If we truly believe it is not God's will, then we need to accept responsibility for allowing this to exist in the world God blessed us with and recommended to our care.

Our GPS (God's Plan for Salvation) points us toward our destination, where we are ultimately directed, which grows clearer as we approach and are able to detect more details of that goal: living harmonious relationships (on all four levels: with God, ourselves, others, and nature).

The Ideal Toward Which We Strive: Harmony

Living in harmony implies sharing. Since we each have something unique to offer, and we all need one another, we cannot write anyone off, leave them behind, or exclude them. That provokes an imbalance and rupture in God's plan for us. Harmony requires working to restore some of the balance indicated in God's plan: enough for all forever.

Spiritual poverty (far from the mistaken notion of a deficiency of faith or an unhealthy relationship with God) means recognizing that all is gift, given to me but not for me, rather to share, just as God freely shares it with me.

Spiritual poverty is grace, received with gratitude, graciously bestowed, not purchased, nor deserved, merited, or warranted. Grace is freely given not because you or I deserve it but because God is good, wants what is best for us, but will always allow us to choose what we believe to be best for us.

Spiritual poverty is utter, absolute reliance not on my bank account or degree, but on God. It depends on our capacity to resist the temptation to accumulate, to assure our own security at any price, which ultimately comes from the desire to be God, to be in control, to be self-sufficient. The goal is neither dependence nor independence but interdependence, emphasizing mutuality.

Spiritual poverty allows us to recognize that all we have and are is gift, given freely and generously by a loving and compassionate God. God created everything for everybody. Spiritual poverty is good.

Material poverty is definitely not good; spiritual poverty is appreciated and prized. The path from where we are presently toward where we and God would like us to be (harmonious relationships) passes through voluntary poverty.

Voluntary poverty (sometimes called solidarity) is a way of actualizing spiritual poverty—a very positive development—choosing to live simply so that others can simply live: using wisely, sharing generously, avoiding accumulation. It is a way to honor God in one another, whose temples we have become. A way of living voluntary poverty is to choose austerity, to live simply, without accumulating things in order to assuage our inner deserts. Austerity is not the same as material poverty. Austerity is a strategy for living voluntary poverty.

Recognizing that all we have and are is truly gift, voluntary poverty involves willingly assuming the condition of those who have been left out, often identified with the preferential option for the poor, the materially poor. To try to see the world through the eyes of the poor is incarnational theology, which helps us understand Jesus' place of birth, where he was brought up, and how he died.

Voluntary poverty means sharing who I am and what I have with others, just as many parents and grandparents, aunts and uncles, neighbors and friends do. We recognize that we are called to exercise voluntary poverty with all members of the human family, without conditions or limits, just as God does with us.

This is the path chosen by Jesus in word and deed, appropriated by those who choose to follow Jesus' example, much as Augustine did when he returned to Africa and gathered around himself his first community. He asked all who wanted to live with him to voluntarily divest themselves of their property, to put it in common, in order to serve the needs of all, beginning with their own community but reaching out to attend to the needs of the materially poor.

Sharing involves spiritual poverty and voluntary poverty as concrete expressions of the profound desire to overcome material poverty. We understand sharing as a way of being in the world, for a better world for all, of living in harmonious relationships, offering prophetic witness of the beloved community. Holding things in common is part and parcel of this life together, which Jesus and his close followers modeled for the world.

Not only Augustinian friars, nor just religious men and women, but also all who choose to participate in Jesus' mission to announce in word and deed the presence of the reign of God among us, by living now in anticipation as we believe we are all called to live forever, as prophetic witness in the world, for a better world, for all. Our way of expressing that goal, the horizon toward which we endeavor, which God longs to see become a reality, is "enough for all forever." Voluntary poverty, or sharing, marks the path that lifts us all up together.

"Enough" implies balance and harmony, not equal portions but equitable proportions, according to each one's need. What is enough for me might not be for you, and what God searches for us is abundant life for all. This involves everyone working as hard as they can, not in competition but in collaboration, for we each have different abilities and limitations. It is in sharing the load that we come to understand the significance of living in harmony.

Equality is not the same as equity; equality would mean we all have the same abilities and appetites. Equity allows for and rejoices in the diversity of God's creation, with appreciation for how the different parts of the body work together in harmony, each one contributing from their own identity.

That abundant life or living in harmony we frequently call eternal life, which might, mistakenly, cause us to think that it is after life, when we know that it is meant to begin here and now, in this life. The reign of God was announced and inaugurated by Jesus. Those who choose to follow Jesus share his mission to build up the reign of God here and now.

Jesus affirmed: I came that you might have life and have it more abundantly. By proclaiming that, he was not promising pie in the sky, not postponing justifiable recompense, not encouraging us to accept and assume suffering now to enjoy rewards later.

Indeed, this is good news for those who have been left out, excluded, and banished. It is also not so good news for those who are satisfied, who are considered important to society, who close the door on those outside—the me-firsters.

All are invited, all are encouraged, all can choose to promote the common good, for our common home. Augustine speaks in this chapter of food, clothing, books, and material goods in the context of the common good. We redefine those items by enlarging the scope to include the environment in general.

We are all called to contribute to a healthier environment, to the common good, which provides an overall atmosphere that makes evident God's concern for all, for each one, but also for the totality: those alive now and those yet to be born, those in wealthy nations or regions, and those who suffer want and misery.

The path includes the challenge to reduce, renew, refurbish, restore, recycle, and repurpose what exists to move it toward what we believe God wants all of us to be: one family, one common home. The idea behind the circular economy is that we stop discarding what we consider waste until we reach a society that doesn't accumulate waste at all. But what methods do we use to achieve this?

Reduce, renew, refurbish, restore, repurpose, and recycle are all strategies to promote a circular economy. All relate to extending the lifespan and use of materials, but with slightly different nuances.

- Reduce: The idea behind reduce is that what never is, can never be waste. We can make cars more and more energy efficient, with electric cars slowly becoming more common, but the best thing for the environment is not to have a car at all if you don't need it. Austerity and simplicity are brought to bear.

- Renew implies giving something a fresh start or a new lease on life, often in a spiritual or personal sense. Instead of repairing what is broken, it is also possible to take the working parts of a broken device and use them for something new.

- Refurbish means to renovate or repair something, bringing it back to a usable state. This means that we must keep using things as long as possible, carefully maintaining them, till they really do not function anymore.

- Restore implies returning something to its original condition, like repairing a historical building.

- Repurpose means using something for a different purpose than it was originally intended, like turning an old chair into a bookshelf.

- Recycle means taking something apart until you get back the original resources you used to make it; these can then be used to make new products and parts from scratch. This can be something entirely different!

The Ideal Toward Which We Strive: Harmony

Much as we are called to be the People of God, represented better by a circle in which all are equidistant and all participate in composing the whole, so too, in a circular economy, at the service of the planet and of all people, we collaborate in building and sustaining what God has created for the benefit of all.

Saint Augustine, reflecting on the Christian community described in the Acts of the Apostles, realistically expects diversity. He likewise promotes harmony, by which differences are respected and, under the influence of grace, the community approaches unity.

Our unity as a community of faith is not self-centered, nor is it an end in itself. It is fundamentally outward-directed toward God as the goal. Harmony is not understood as uniformity, but rather the effective blending of differences.

Like the community of Acts, we are called to be wise stewards of our time, treasure, and talents—both material and spiritual goods. Freed from the burden of possessiveness, Augustine encourages us to abandon all self-seeking to find joy in sharing with others God's manifold gifts. The community can hold goods in common, and from this storehouse share whatever is necessary for those in need. Our communities advance this way of life by embracing stewardship, sharing with others what has been freely shared with us, and focusing our mission on the genuine concern for those who are in need, freely and ungrudgingly offering to attend to the needs of others.

When common resources are joyfully shared to meet individual needs, the community itself is strengthened, both the person providing the resources and the one receiving the benefits. This reflects the life of our Trinitarian God, in our limitation of God's own generosity and sharing. The core teaching of the Gospel and the first principle of social justice is that every human person is a child of God, worthy of respect and dignity. An Augustinian community encourages each person to use their God-given gifts in service to the broader community.

The Practice of Prayer in Common

Another Vignette to Set the Scene on This Topic

On a recent Saturday morning, I was walking into the parish church where my sister's community worships (she is a Dominican sister in Blauvelt, NY) for the 8 a.m. Mass. At the door of the church, I noticed an elderly couple and simply said good morning and continued up the main aisle.

    Suddenly, from the back of the church, I heard a shout: Eddie! Since that's not my name, I simply continued up the aisle to find a seat. But then, insistently, and very loudly, I heard again: Eddie! So I turned around and looked back to the doorway and saw the elderly couple waving at me! Puzzled, I looked closer and recognized my next-door neighbor from when I was a child in the Bronx, Mrs. Kivlehan.

I hadn't seen her, and she hadn't seen me, since my parents moved from the Bronx some forty years previously. And although my name is not Eddie, it is my father's name, and it struck me: She thinks I am my father!

I rushed back to the doorway and greeted her effusively, making sure she knew I was Arthur, that Eddie was my father, who long ago had passed away.

The greeting was sweet, but the effects long-lasting: She thought I was my father! Something in the way I walked, how I greeted her, something readily identifiable to her made her think I was my father.

I was and am so proud that someone would confuse me with my dad, a great person, but then I thought: Would anyone really confuse me with my heavenly Father! Now that would be something to aspire to!

The Rule of Augustine, Chapter 2

10. "Persevere faithfully in prayer" at the hours and times appointed.

11. The place of prayer should not be used for any purpose other than that for which it is intended and from which it takes its name. Thus, if someone wants to pray there even outside the appointed hours, in his own free time, he should be able to do so without being hindered by others who have no business being there.

12. When you pray to God in psalms and songs, the words spoken by your lips should also be alive in [your] heart.

13. When you sing, keep to the text you have, and [do] not sing what is not intended to be sung.

―――·•••·―――

Personal prayer, between God and myself, is the fruit of my other relationships and opens me up to them. By nature, we are social beings, created in the image and likeness of a Trinitarian God. We are called to grow in and deepen those relationships. Our personal communication with God and in God is one of the great sources of that growth. We become more like God to the extent that we go out of ourselves to enter into communion with others and creation itself. Our personal prayer is not meant to be individual prayer, isolated, separate from who I am in relation to others and nature.

Community prayer, or prayer in common, is quite distinct from personal prayer, which is important in and of itself but cannot be presumed, since we cannot have true communal prayer without a strong personal prayer practice.

Augustine spoke directly to his local community on this topic, assuming that their personal prayer was already in place. It would be wise to remember that the community Augustine was addressing was far from uniform: the social, economic, and cultural background was quite diverse, as must have been the expectations of each of the community members. That diversity could very readily enrich the community prayer, opening minds and hearts to the vast treasure of God's holiness, viewed from such diverse backgrounds.

In five brief sentences (comprising the shortest of the eight chapters of *The Rule* he left us), Augustine touches on four major concerns in the prayer life of this community called to live in harmony.

Spirituality

Those of you involved in marathons know well the importance of proper training. Some may have a natural propensity for running at great speed, others for long distances, almost no one—I presume—is ready to run a marathon distance at the drop of a hat. Training takes time, patience, dedication, discipline, and a strong desire to achieve the goal you assume for yourself.

Community prayer requires dedication, discipline, training, and time, similar to marathoners. Eyes on the prize: deeper relations on all four levels, to become more like God.

The principal image of God I hold in my mind and heart may very well not be the same one I held five years ago, or five months ago, or even five minutes ago. Since this relationship with God is personal, it may vary with the time of day, diet, and health, as well as with how I am dealing with others or with nature (think of a gloomy, rainy day and how it can affect your state of mind). All four levels of relationship (with God, self, others, and nature) are called into play in the dynamic of prayer, particularly in community prayer.

In order to share prayer with others, an agreed-upon time and format are necessary, as well as accepted norms and practices. Ideally, these are reviewed and decided through dialogue in community and periodic evaluations. A quick appraisal might be that if our community prayer is the same today as it was five years ago . . . why would that be? Are you wearing the same clothes, watching the same programs, reading the same book . . .? Don't we grow, personally and communally? Well, then, it might be healthy to consider how we pray together; how is it helping us to grow, to listen, and respond to the ever-changing signs of the times, to take into account our age and ministry profiles, theological trends, and pastoral tendencies.

If we truly share prayer in community, then we want the fruit of our personal prayer to be brought to bear as we pray together. This involves a willingness to listen, the ability to articulate what I think and feel, to adapt, and to grow together (which is very different from growing apart or separately).

Our spirituality is a sharing in the spirit and sanctity of God, which no one person can aspire to attain, but rather all are called to enjoy in community, as we share our own particular blessings and insights from our personal identities. We grow more, mature more, become more sanctified to the extent that we go out of ourselves to enter into communion with God, with others, and with nature, as Pope Francis reminded us in *Laudato si'* (no. 240).

Mass, by its very nature, is an exercise in community prayer, although some worshippers tend to highlight an individualistic relationship with God through personal devotional practices during these communal prayers. How can we help improve ongoing formation to have better communal worship practices?

We might do well, also, to heed the advice of Pope Francis regarding thanksgiving prayer at mealtime, an appropriate time and place to recognize God's providence and our dependency. A meal is a community exercise (it takes a village, so to speak): those who plant, harvest, package, ship, sell, prepare, eat, and clean up. We can bring all those people who have collaborated to our table by recalling their contributions to our meal.

The Place in Which the Community Prays

As I write these words, I find myself in the Augustinian monastery in San Gimignano, in Tuscany, built in 1279, and inhabited by many different groups of friars and laity throughout the centuries. Many return here year after year, or occasionally, to enjoy the accumulated holiness that resides within this cloister and chapel. So many have worshipped together here, in so many diverse languages, from many different cultures, in various styles and formats, all communing with and in our common Parent and Creator.

Spaces and places can foster and encourage holiness. From the time of Augustine, sixteen centuries ago, Augustinian houses have been encouraged to designate a special place for prayer, as many families do as well. The physical space is at least a reminder that God resides with us, is never far from us, and longs to be present to us. We reserve a place for the communal worship of God because we know we need God, and we are humbled by God choosing to need us to continue his Son's mission: to announce in word and deed the good news that God is near, loves, forgives, and embraces us.

At another point in time, over twenty years ago, I had the great pleasure and privilege to reside for a month and a half in Annaba, ancient Hippo, located in what is now Algeria, in Northern Africa, where I replaced one of our friars so he could visit his family. While I was there, busy writing my doctoral thesis, I had the chance each day to visit the site of the ruins of Hippo, which date back to the time of Augustine, and enter the remaining walls of the Basilica of Peace, where Augustine worshipped and preached. I would sit in the stone seat, or cathedra, still in the place it was when Augustine would sit there and preach during the last thirty-eight years of his life. How familiar he was to the people and how close they were to him.

Those ruins helped all the sermons of Augustine I read while in Annaba come to life: the foibles and fancies he talked about, the devotions and testimony he witnessed. Even more so, it helped bring to life the chapters of *The Rule* written in Annaba before the year 400, which make mention of physical spaces that are readily identifiable even sixteen centuries later. What a holy place, so significant, so meaningful.

So too, for each of us, in our own community, be it a friary or a convent, an apartment or our family home: a place and space to experience together the God who chooses to remain close to us, reminding us of his love, and his need of us. How we cherish and care for this space, how we adorn it with flowers or plants, mementoes and lights, will say much to those who are aware of its existence. Sharing with guests and visitors the space and the reason for it will also communicate much about our God and who we are.

Wouldn't it be wonderful if we could extend that care and concern to the surrounding spaces as well: sharing a lawn mower with neighbors, shoveling the snow from someone else's sidewalk or porch, providing a plant or flowers to someone who is bedridden, sharing a meal or vegetables, encouraging a community garden to be able to share in a local soup kitchen. So many ways to make holy spaces part of our life and our neighborhood.

Perhaps we could also contemplate the possibility of programming opportunities for members of the family or neighbors to pray in nature, designating a natural space in the garden or park as a regular place for praying. This could be accompanied by recording and sharing with others these moments of encounter with God in nature.

Authenticity and Sincerity in Prayer: Meditating in the Heart on What Is Expressed by Our Lips

Did you ever stop to think how many times you've prayed the Our Father on a particular day or week? Not a highly productive exercise, giving mathematics some undeserved attention or weight. Repeating words, mouthing phrases, simply does not add up to communal prayer.

The Practice of Prayer in Common

Praying together involves intention and awareness, a conscious decision to place our mind and heart in the presence of God, to commit ourselves to help one another remain faithful to this exercise, to seek and want together what God wants. Voicing the same words, repetitive prayer, can be conducive to uniting our minds and hearts, as experience proves. But it can also, on occasion, be a frustratingly mindless exercise, distracting rather than promoting communal prayer. To mean what we say and to say what we mean requires focus, intentionality, concentration, and divine inspiration.

What a wonderful gift it is to encounter a few moments of absolute silence, without being interrupted by a phone ringing, an ambulance or fire engine clanging on its sacred mission. The joy of being able to hear the birds chirping, the wind rushing through the leaves, and to notice the scent of flowers in the air! These moments are always available; they simply require our undivided attention to become aware of the gift God has prepared for us to enjoy.

So too, with the words we repeat in prayer, the thoughts and images they can evoke and capture, the meaning they are capable of communicating, if we only take the time to pay attention. This might mean praying at a different pace, intentionally slowing down in order to savor the words and bask in their significance as we pray in community. Singing or chanting is a time-honored method to help us think about the sounds we are making, the significance of each syllable, the impact of each word, the continuity leading to wholeness.

Prayer Needs to Be Purposeful, Not Rote or Mindless

I don't know if this happens to you, but not infrequently, I find that when I am ready to clean up after a snack or a meal, I stand in front of the varied colored bins trying to decide in which trash bin each item needs to be deposited. I'm in a rush, wanting to move on swiftly to the next thing on my agenda, and I can't spend time trying to figure out what to do with my waste!

Concern for the needs of the poor, as well as those of the planet, encourages me to take the time to learn how not only to reduce waste but also to place what is truly waste in the appropriate container. I can make this a moment of prayer, when I raise my mind and heart to God, to appreciate what has been shared with me and to consider how I can best care for what is left over. This can become more than an individual activity; it invites me to make of it something personal, understood as relational, caring for others as well as for nature itself, something I can share or do with others, recognizing in humility my need for help.

Waste is inconsiderate of future generations as well as of those who are currently deprived of the rudimentary means for living a fully human life. Our commitment to live in harmony obliges us to take waste into account, our own and that of others. It also compels us to overcome the temptation to mindlessly repeat accepted practices so that we can intentionally advance the cause of the poor and the planet, both now and in the future.

Augustine's admonition to not sing what is not intended to be sung can readily be reinterpreted in our time to refer to other forms of waste: time, food, energy, attention . . . He prescribes keeping to the text we have, attentively, not embellishing what does not need or call for embellishment. This would not be welcome advice on the menu of most of our upscale restaurants. Keep it simple, nourishing, and pleasant, but avoid waste.

Too much depends on our ability to share what God freely shares with us: All that we have and are may be considered gifts to be shared.

The community is always called to have an outward focus, seeking and finding Christ in others. Allowance for personal and private prayer is contemplated so that the God who dwells within can be found. Prayer and liturgy encourage a peaceful and harmonious community. For authentic community life to exist, there must be a faith-based sharing of one's interior life as we journey on our way to God. Our prayer together must come from the heart, contemplating in our hearts what is pronounced by our lips.

To those four major concerns of Augustine related to community prayer, allow me to call your attention to another aspect of prayer that was very close to his heart: Sabbath, or rest.

The Practice of Prayer in Common

In the very first paragraph of Augustine's *Confessions*, we are invited into the prayer that contains one of the most celebrated phrases he ever uttered:

> Great are you, O Lord, and exceedingly worthy of praise . . . You stir us so that praising you may bring us joy, because you have made us and drawn us to yourself, and our heart is restless until it rests in you. (chapter 1, no. 1)

Then, in the final book of the *Confessions*, in the closing paragraphs, Augustine again invites us into his prayer of praise:

> Give us peace, Lord God, for you have given us all else; give us the peace that is repose, the peace of the Sabbath, and the peace that knows no evening . . . when our works are finished, we too may rest in you, in the Sabbath of eternal life . . . And then you will rest in us, as now you work in us . . . we hope that we shall rest in your immense holiness. (XIII, 50, 51, 52, 53)

Keeping the Sabbath—understood as calling to mind and memorializing God's resting on the seventh day of creation—can be important for keeping the Earth healthy! Observing the Sabbath, a day of rest and reflection, can positively impact our relationship with the environment and encourage more sustainable practices.

The idea of Sabbath is to intentionally slow down in order to appreciate the gift of creation and to take time to re-evaluate priorities, which can lead to a more balanced and environmentally conscious lifestyle. Resting on the Sabbath can involve not buying anything, not cleaning the house, or balancing the checkbook, which positively translates into time to enjoy the family, the neighborhood, take a walk, read, and relax.

By intentionally slowing down and reducing consumption on the Sabbath, we can also contribute to decreased energy use and waste. Keeping the Sabbath can lead to a greater awareness of our impact on the environment and a desire to make more sustainable choices in other areas of life.

Living Simply, in Harmony, to Share

Setting the Scene with Another Vignette: Petronila of Pacaipampa

As alien as the experience of my family in the Bronx in the era of the 1950s might seem to you, even more challenging will it be to identify with Petronila, an elderly grandmother native to the extremely small village (one among ninety-six such villages that comprise the territory of the parish) high up (more than 6,500 feet above sea level) in the Andes of Pacaipampa, Peru. Yet I don't want to deprive you of this great witness, who reveals to me so clearly the maternal image of God.

Petronila lives in a small hut with her daughter, who was abandoned by her husband, and her two grandchildren. They eat what they grow, rarely being able to barter and trade some of their meager produce with other farming families not too far away, who happen to grow something different. No electricity, no running water, no medical attention, no heat, and only recently, graced with a one-room schoolhouse for all six grades of primary school, a mere forty-five-minute walk from their home. The teacher arrives on Monday and returns to her village on Friday, so even the meager education possible is abbreviated.

Petronila has grown accustomed to walking her two grandchildren to this community-built schoolhouse each day, Monday through Friday, waiting there until their classes end, and then walking them back home again.

She manages to look after the few sheep in the family flock as well as shearing their wool, spinning it into threads, whether walking or sitting, then weaving these threads into clothing, a poncho, a bookbag, or a lunch bag for the children. As she spins, she is thinking of that person she is making this item for: her daughter or one of the grandchildren, for some special neighbor perhaps. Thinking, dreaming, hoping, and wishing the future recipient well.

Petronila brings to mind the God who thought of me before I was in my mother's womb, spinning the many threads of my ancestors into my existence, dreaming of me, of what I could be.

Petronila lives for her family, looks after each of them, cares for them, nurses them when needed, coddles them whenever possible, wants to make their life easier, more enjoyable, more joyful. She makes sure they have something to eat, something to drink, and some way of knowing they are each important and worthy of her attention.

Petronila is close, never far from any one of the family members, aware of their needs and concerns, available to chat or help with some task, to encourage, to celebrate, to rejoice, to sympathize. Petronila is the feminine, maternal face of God.

The Rule of Augustine, **Chapter 3**

14. As far as your health allows, keep your bodily appetites in check by fasting and abstinence from food and drink. Those who are unable to fast the whole day may have something to eat before

the main meal, which takes place in the late afternoon. They may do this, however, only around midday. But the sick may have something to eat any time of day.

15. From the beginning of the meal to the end, listen to the customary reading without noise or protest against Scriptures, for you have not only to satisfy your physical hunger, but also "to hunger for the Word of God."

16. There are some who are weaker because of their former manner of life. If an exception is made for them at table, those who are stronger because they have come from a different way of life ought not to take this amiss or to consider it unfair. They should not think that the others are more fortunate because they are capable of something [that] is beyond the strength of the others.

17. There are some who, before entering the religious life, were accustomed to living comfortably, and therefore they have received something more in the way of food and clothing: better bedding perhaps, or more blankets. The others who are stronger, and therefore happier, do not receive these things. But, taking into account the former habits of life of the rich, keep in mind how much they now have to do without, even though they cannot live as simply as those who are physically stronger. Not everyone should want to have the extra he sees another receive, for this is done not to show favor but only out of concern for the person. Otherwise, deplorable disorder would creep into religious life, whereby the poor begin to drift easily along while the rich put themselves out in every possible way.

18. The sick should obviously receive suitable food; otherwise, their illness would only get worse. Once they are over the worst of their sickness, they ought to be well-cared for so that they may be fully restored to health as quickly as possible. And this holds good even if they formerly belonged to the very poorest class in society. During their convalescence they should receive the

same care that the rich are entitled to because of their former manner of life. But once they have made a complete recovery they are to go back to living as they did earlier on, when they were happier because their needs were fewer. The simpler [the] way of life, the better it is suited to servants of God.

―――・・・・・―――

Petronila helps us understand who God is, as Jesus knew God and revealed God to us. How wonderful to know that we are not alone, that there is someone thinking of us, looking after us, caring for us, wanting to help us, longing to embrace us. That is Jesus' experience, and I hope and pray that it is also mine and yours.

We are all worthy of God's love, each one of us, all of us, the whole person, just as we are, not merely as we wish we could be. This, too, is our role in the world: to be Petronila for others, excluding no one, embracing everyone, coddling them into a smile, a hint of happiness and joy.

Abundant life, to the extent that Petronila knows it, is certainly not the rat race that some learn to negotiate and call "life": caring more about what others think of me than what I think of myself; being goaded into sacrificing my closest relationships in order to work and earn enough to have more possessions to take care of; trying out the latest diet, following the most recent workout, taking all the pills needed to keep anxiety down, depression at bay, insomnia tamed, stomach acid in place.

In Petronila's experience, everything is truly interrelated: plants and animals, people and nature, sunshine and rain, sickness and health, joy and sorrow, life and death. We all need each other, we are better together than alone. If we search for meaning in life, we certainly won't find it in just accumulating material things.

The *Compendium of the Social Doctrine of the Church* was published by the Vatican in 2004, at the request of Pope John Paul II, in order to give a concise but complete overview of the Church's social teaching. In that document, we find these thoughts on *dignity*, the fundamental principle of Catholic social teaching:

- The relationship between God and man is reflected in the relational and social dimension of human nature. Man and woman are in relationship with others, above all, as those to whom the lives of others have been entrusted. With this specific vocation to life, man and woman find themselves also in the presence of all the other creatures. They can and are obliged to put them at their own service and to enjoy them, but their dominion over the world requires the exercise of responsibility; it is not a freedom of arbitrary and selfish exploitation. All of creation in fact has value and is "good" in the sight of God, who is its author. (nos. 110, 112, 113)

- Man is also in relationship with himself and is able to reflect on himself. Sacred Scripture speaks in this regard about the heart of man. The heart designates man's inner spirituality, what distinguishes him from every other creature. (no. 114)

- A just society can become a reality only when it is based on the respect of the transcendent dignity of the human person. The person represents the ultimate end of society, by which it is ordered to the person: "Hence, the social order and its development must invariably work to the benefit of the human person, since the order of things is to be subordinate to the order of persons, and not the other way around." (no. 132)

- Authentic social changes are effective and lasting only to the extent that they are based on resolute changes in personal conduct. "God shows no partiality," since all people have the same dignity as creatures made in his image and likeness. Since something of the glory of God shines on the face of every person, the dignity of every person before God is the basis of the dignity of man before other men. Only the recognition of human dignity can make possible the common and personal growth of everyone. (nos. 134, 144, 145; See also nos. 105-149)

Living Simply, in Harmony, to Share

Respect for the dignity of each and every human being is not something granted or conceded to us by our constitution or legislature. It is a gift of God and belongs to all. Dignity cannot be legislated, but respect for our dignity can be promoted and guaranteed by legislation.

We, as People of God and Church are called to give witness to the values God has shared with us. Dignity tells me that no one is so poor that they have nothing to offer or share. But also that no one is so rich that they do not need others to grow.

Dignity in a society that values people for what they possess rather than for who they are is out of balance, in discordance with our beliefs. Our structures, our society, and our economy reflect our values, or those very structures begin to break down, in order to allow our genuine values to be manifested.

Everything is interconnected; all creation is interrelated. Pope Francis never tired of reminding us of this basic belief, precisely because of the ever-increasing individualism and debilitating isolation in our world. Pope Leo has taken up the cry, promoting ever-deeper and more meaningful relationships as a path toward the better world designed by God from the beginning, but thwarted by our own selfishness and greed, which confuses having more with being more. The desire to possess more, even at the expense of others having less, even if that means leaving some—too many—to endure subhuman conditions, rather than sharing more so that all can thrive, is the motor of our economy, what makes our marketplace.

Once again, Pope Francis articulates what we know in our hearts:

> The external deserts in the world are growing, because the internal deserts have become so vast. Our inner desert grows to the extent that we place our trust in material goods to provide a sense of fulfillment, rather than by fostering our relationships. (*Laudato si'*, no. 217)

For this reason, the ecological crisis is also a summons to profound interior conversion. This conversion calls for attitudes that foster a spirit of generous care, full of tenderness. First, it entails gratitude and gratuitousness, a recognition that the world is God's loving gift, and that we are called quietly to imitate his generosity in self-sacrifice and good works.

Augustine's *Rule* can be characterized as promoting a community witness of the lifestyle of the early Christian community of Jerusalem (Acts 2 and 4) to a society clearly disfigured by possessiveness, where private property is unhampered by any social responsibility, where consumerism, materialism, pride, arrogance, and seeking power over others are given free rein.

As such, *The Rule* offers an implicit protest against discrimination and inequality in society, offering as a counterweight an alternative way of life characterized by the sharing of goods, both material and spiritual.

In contemporary culture, our salaries indicate how much we are worth, and so many (too many) earn so little. The most promising approach to eradicating poverty and eliminating disparities associated with race, disability, and diversity is to promote respect for the dignity of each and every human being. We each are a gift to one another! Dignity is the issue, not money, not any program, or law.

From this foundational principle of the dignity of each and every human being, the Church derives the principle of the common good. Another way to understand what is meant by the term "common good" is that which I want for myself and am willing to strive for with the same intensity to achieve it for others as well.

Concern for the common good is a major theme of this chapter of *The Rule*, as is the promotion of the sustainability of all creation. Abundant life for all, as Jesus would recommend, is less a matter of equality than of equity, thereby appreciating diversity and personalized attention which flow from our particularly unique identity and the corresponding expression of dignity and value from which each of us is called to contribute to the common good.

Augustine uses the examples of our bodily appetites for food and drink, our preconditioning in regard to comfort and physical labor, and our overall health to support the alternative of leading simple lives, choosing to make do with a little rather than growing accustomed to having too much.

Fasting, abstinence, sacrifice, and self-denial are all necessary for spiritual growth, but they are means, not ends in themselves. Saint Augustine urges moderation in all things, advising spiritual discipline "so far as your health permits." These practices are meant to lead us to God and to living a simple lifestyle, rejecting materialism and consumerism to be in solidarity with the poor. In the words of Augustine: "It is better for us to want a little than to have too much."

Private property is a major topic in contemporary society and, from the perspective of faith, is considered within the context of the universal destination of goods by the Catholic Church's social doctrine. Because private property is so significant in our society, and yet so misunderstood within the context of our faith, we examine church teaching in this regard with the following paragraphs from the *Compendium of the Social Doctrine of the Church*:

- Private property and other forms of private ownership of goods "assure a person a highly necessary sphere for the exercise of his personal and family autonomy and ought to be considered as an extension of human freedom . . . stimulating exercise of responsibility, it constitutes one of the conditions for civil liberty." Private property is an essential element of an authentically social and democratic economic policy, and it is the guarantee of a correct social order. The Church's social doctrine requires that ownership of goods be equally accessible to all, so that all may become, at least in some measure, owners, and it excludes recourse to forms of "common and promiscuous dominion." (no. 176)

- Christian tradition has never recognized the right to private property as absolute and untouchable: "On the contrary, it has always understood this right within the broader context of the right common to all to use the goods of the whole of creation: the right to private property is subordinated to the right to common use, to the fact that goods are meant for everyone." The principle of the universal destination of goods is an affirmation both of God's full and perennial lordship over every reality and of the requirement that the goods of creation remain ever destined to the development of the whole person and of all humanity. This principle is not opposed to the right to private property but indicates the need to regulate it.Private property, in fact, regardless of the concrete forms of the regulations and juridical norms relative to it, is in its essence only an instrument for respecting the principle of the universal destination of goods; in the final analysis, therefore, it is not an end but a means. (no. 177)

- The Church's social teaching moreover calls for recognition of the social function of any form of private ownership that clearly refers to its necessary relation to the common good. Man "should regard the external things that he legitimately possesses not only as his own but also as common in the sense that they should be able to benefit not only him but also others." Individual persons may not use their resources without considering the effects that this use will have, rather they must act in a way that benefits not only themselves and their family but also the common good. (no. 178)

- The right to private property is subordinated to the principle of the universal destination of goods and must not constitute a reason for impeding the work or development of others. Property, which is acquired in the first place through work, must be placed at the service of work. (no. 282)

What a Waste! Live Simply in Order to Share

Households are responsible for about one-third of the food waste on our planet. Coincidentally, about one-third of the world's population goes to bed hungry every evening. You can see where this is going: we can do something about food waste, and it involves sharing.

Consumers, collectively, are responsible for more wasted food than farmers, grocery stores, restaurants, or any other part of the food chain. The average family in the United States today wastes 50 percent more food than forty years ago, and the trend is not improving. Great Britain, on the other hand, has turned that trend around by 18 percent in the last five years. Doing the same in the United States would mean a savings of hundreds of dollars per family each year.

Morally and economically, it's a no-brainer. Awareness is the first step; now it's time to take action. Fresh vegetables are the largest source of food waste, money thrown in the garbage, literally. They are followed by fish and meat, then dairy products.

Check your fridge and plan your meals before shopping. Use up leftovers. Serve smaller portions. If you need to throw food out, compost (the average family in the United States throws out an estimated $150 a month in spoiled and discarded food).

We lift up our mind and heart with the words Augustine wrote sixteen centuries ago in Africa in appreciation for what God prepared for each one and all of us to enjoy:

> Just think of the world in which we live! Think of the thousands of beautiful things for seeing and the thousands of materials just right for making things. There is an infinitely changing beauty in the sky and the land and the sea. What varieties of color do we see in the changing moon and sun and stars! There are the soft shadows of forests at noon, the shades and smells of spring flowers, the different songs and exotic dresses of the birds. How amazing are the animals who surround us, the smallest ant even more amazing than the huge bulk of the whale!

Living Simply, in Harmony, to Share

Think of the grand spectacle of the sea as it clothes itself in different colors, sometimes green, sometimes purple, sometimes the bluest of blue. And how grand it is when there is a storm (especially grand when you are not sailing on the heaving surface of the sea but are caressed by its soft mist as you stand safe and warm on the shore). (*The City of God*, 22, 24)

Mutual Responsibility for Growing in Harmonious Living

Gerard Manley Hopkins, S.J., provides an opening to the topic of this chapter of *The Rule* in light of the challenge of integral ecology.

The world is charged with the grandeur of God.
It will flame out, like shining from shook foil;
It gathers to a greatness, like the ooze of oil
Crushed. Why do men then now not reck his rod?
Generations have trod, have trod, have trod;
And all is seared with trade; bleared, smeared with toil;
And wears man's smudge and shares man's smell: the soil
Is bare now, nor can foot feel, being shod.

And for all this, nature is never spent;
There lives the dearest freshness deep down things;
And though the last lights off the black West went
Oh, morning, at the brown brink eastward, springs—
Because the Holy Ghost over the bent

> *World broods with warm breast and with*
> *ah! bright wings. (God's Grandeur)*

The world, creation itself, is alive, on fire with God's grandeur: We can perceive God's hand in so much of nature. But to be charged also involves being responsible for creation, involved in the process and in the care of our common home: to be both blessed with and responsible for creation, gift of God!

We have the immense privilege as well as weighty responsibility as persons and people to build a better world that will make it easier to recognize the hand of God, the generous plan for abundant life for all, forever.

In his *Confessions*, Augustine treats of how marvelous he finds God's creation as well as the need to be faithful stewards of the gifts of creation, particularly in view of the evident brokenness, which our arrogance has caused. And yet he was able to articulate:

> This is what I love when I love my God. And what is this? I put my question to the earth and it replied 'I am not he'; I questioned everything it held, and they confessed the same. I questioned the sea and the great deep, and the teeming live creatures that crawl, and they replied, 'We are not God; seek higher.' . . . And to all things which stood around the portals of my flesh I said: 'Tell me of my God. You are not he, but tell me something of him.' Then they lifted up their voices and cried: 'He made us.'
> (*Confessions* X, vi)

Both Augustine and Gerard Manley Hopkins recognize the interdependence and interference of humanity in nature. Both are able to see beyond smeared creation to redemption. Our selfishness and pride certainly manage to damage but cannot obstruct "God's Grandeur".

The Rule of Augustine, Chapter 4

19. Do not attract attention by the way [you] dress. Endeavor to impress by your manner of life, not by the clothes you wear.

20. When you go out, go with somebody else, and stay together when you have reached your destination.

21. Whatever you are doing, your behavior should in no way cause offense to anyone, but should rather be in keeping with the holiness of your way of life.

22. When you see a woman, do not keep provocatively looking at her. Of course, no one can forbid you to see women when you go out, "but it is wrong to desire a woman or to want her to desire you." For it is not only by affectionate embraces that desire between man and woman is awakened, but also by looks. You cannot say that your inner attitude is good if, with your eyes, you desire to possess a woman; for the eye is the herald of the heart. And if people allow their impure intentions to appear, albeit without words, but just looking at each other and finding pleasure in each other's passion, even though not in each other's arms, we cannot speak any longer of true chastity, which is precisely that of the heart.

23. Indeed, if a person cannot keep his eyes off of a woman and enjoys attracting her attention, he should not imagine that others do not see this. Of course, they see it; even people [who] you would not expect to, notice it. But even if it did remain concealed and unseen by men, will it not be seen by "God who scans the heart of every man" and from whom nothing is hidden? Or are we to imagine that "God does not see it" because just as his wisdom is far beyond ours, so too is he prepared to be extraordinarily patient with us? A religious should be afraid "to offend the God of love," and for the sake of this love, he ought to be ready to give up a sinful love for a woman. Whoever is mindful that God sees all things will not wish to look at a woman with sinful desire. For, precisely on this point, the text of Scripture, "the Lord abhors a covetous eye," impresses on us that we are to stand in awe of him.

24. Therefore, in church or wherever you may be in the company of women, you are to consider yourselves responsible for one another's chastity. Then "God who dwells in you" will watch over you through your responsibility for one another.

25. If you notice in a brother this provocative look I have spoken of, then warn him immediately, so that the evil that has taken root may not worsen and so that he may promptly improve his behavior.

26. If, after this admonition, you see him doing the same thing again, anyone who notices it should consider him a sick person in need of treatment. At that time, nobody is any longer free to be silent. "First inform one or two others of the situation so that with two or three you will be able to convince him of his fault," and to call him to order with due firmness. Do not think that you are acting out of ill will in doing this. On the contrary, you would be at fault if, by your silence, you allow your brothers to meet their downfall, when by speaking you could set them on the right path.

27. If he does not wish to listen to your warning, then first advise the superior so that he and the brother may talk the matter out in private, and in this way, others will not need to know of it or be involved. If he is still unwilling to listen, then you may bring in others to convince him of his fault. If he still persists in denying it, then, without his knowledge, others must be brought in, so that "his faults may be pointed out" to him "by more than a single witness in the presence of all," for the word of two or three witnesses is more [convincing] than that of one.

Once his guilt has been established, it is up to the superior, or even to the priest under whose jurisdiction the religious house falls, to determine which punishment he should best undergo with a view to his improvement. If he refuses to submit to this punishment, he is to be sent away from the community, even though he himself may be unwilling to go. Here again, this action is not to be prompted by heartlessness but by love, for in this way he is prevented from having a bad influence on others and contributing to their downfall, too.

28. What I have said about looking at a woman lustfully holds too for other sins. In discovering, warding off, bringing to light, proving, and punishing all other faults, you are faithfully and diligently to follow the procedure set out above, always with love for the people involved but with aversion for their faults.

29. If a brother, of his own accord, confesses that he has gone so far along the wrong path as to receive letters and gifts secretly from a woman, we ought to deal with him gently and pray for him. But if he is found out and proved guilty, he is to be severely punished according to the judgment of the priest or superior.

The most outstanding notion of this chapter is its emphasis on mutual responsibility: We are all blessed, and we are all called to be careful of the rest of creation: people, plants, and all of nature.

Augustine reminds us that God, who is within us, will protect us from within ourselves. We are called to discover God in all things, in all people, both in the beauty of creation and in the sighs of the sick, the groans of the afflicted, aware that the life of the spirit is not dissociated from worldly realities.

Living in harmony finds its foundation in the promotion of the dignity of each person, an impossible task without showing concern for the family, groups, associations, local territorial realities; in short, for that aggregate of economic, social, cultural, recreational, professional, and political expressions to which people spontaneously give life and which make it possible for them to achieve effective social growth.

Subsidiarity, among the most constant and characteristic principles of the Church's social doctrine and the standard promoted in this chapter of *The Rule*, involves encouraging active participation in the resolution of our own issues, supporting without supplanting.

The *Compendium of the Social Doctrine of the Church* affirms:

> The principle of subsidiarity protects people from abuse
> by higher-level social authority and calls on these same

authorities to help individuals and intermediate groups to fulfil their duties. This principle is imperative because every person, family and intermediate group has something original to offer to the community. Experience shows that the denial of subsidiarity, or its limitation in the name of an alleged democratization or equality of all members of society, limits and sometimes even destroys the spirit of freedom and initiative. The characteristic implication of subsidiarity is participation, which is a duty to be fulfilled consciously by all, with responsibility and with a view to the common good. (no. 187)

We refer once again to Pope Francis's treatise *On Care for Our Common Home* to bring our attention to the importance of applying the principle of subsidiarity in our interactions.

Underlying the principle of the common good is respect for the human person as such, endowed with basic and inalienable rights ordered to his or her integral development. It has also to do with the overall welfare of society and the development of a variety of intermediate groups, applying the principle of subsidiarity. Outstanding among those groups is the family, as the basic cell of society. Finally, the common good calls for social peace, the stability and security provided by a certain order which cannot be achieved without particular concern for distributive justice; whenever this is violated, violence always ensues. Society as a whole, and the state in particular, are obliged to defend and promote the common good. (no. 157)

Personal agency is paramount in the process of living in harmony, stemming from our fundamental belief in the dignity of each and every human being: We each have something unique to offer, to contribute, to the building up of a better world for all, inaugurated by Jesus and shared with all who choose to join in this mission.

The world itself, as well as each and all of its inhabitants, along with the rest of nature, is charged with the grandeur of God, called to be responsible for caring for and contributing to growth toward wholeness, toward fullness of abundance, toward holiness. We are not alone in this mission; we continue to be accompanied by the one who loves us so much that not only did he give his life for us, but also promised to be with us each day until the end of time.

Together, we build the reign of God, each offering voluntarily from our unique identity, at the invitation of our savior and friend, Jesus, who inaugurated and accompanies this beloved community, inviting us to mutual responsibility for growing in communion.

In this chapter, Augustine reminds his followers throughout the centuries that our behavior should be in keeping with the holiness of our way of life. We are called to stay together, not walk nor work in isolation, not for our own benefit but rather for the common good. Our manner of life, not our clothing, is meant to impress and invite.

It is the God who dwells within us who will watch over us through our mutual responsibility for one another. We all need this mutual support to grow in holiness, to recognize what draws us away from healthy relationships, as well as a commitment to mutual correction to ward off what distracts us from our mission, always out of love for the person and aversion for the fault. We rejoice in our mutual responsibility for growing in love for what is good and in distaste for what detracts and is not done out of love.

Similarly, how much personal hurt could be prevented, how many happy and healthy relationships developed, if we took the time to recognize and appreciate the essential dignity of each person. We have grown so accustomed to purchasing and acquiring, even hoarding objects, storage bins for our private property; it has grown so easy to objectify people as well, considering them as placed here for our benefit, our use, our enjoyment—the throw-away culture at its worst. Pornography allows so many to look at and lust after not someone but some thing, an object of our own pleasure, not a person with whom to enter into a relationship. Ignoring subsidiarity, we want to decide for others, tell them what to do, and make them subservient to our demands.

The flirting alluded to by Augustine in this chapter can be yet another way to elude our responsibility for building a better world for all. Admiration for beauty in all of nature, including in the people we find attractive, or the sense of satisfaction that someone finds me attractive, goes to the heart of the matter: our selfish desire to possess and dominate, to subjugate to our own will, rather than admire and interact with in appreciation for the marvel of God's creation present in each and all of us. We all have something to offer.

Flirting short-circuits that model, wanting my individual (not personal) satisfaction, at any cost to any one else, or any thing else, for that matter (think of oil spills, air contamination, wages unfit for human thriving . . . all to gain, earn, possess more, as though that could make me worth more)! Flirting allows me to project onto you my needs and wants, my desires. I don't need to listen to you, to take you and your wants and needs into account. It's all about me.

Flirting is not the issue here; what really matters is personal and mutual responsibility. We need one another and all of creation in order to grow and become what God gifts to the world through and in each one of us, and all of creation. Using and abusing, objectifying and depersonalizing, facilitate unhealthy relationships. We need one another; we grow together; we build and enjoy better together.

Healthy relationships on all four levels allow God's grandeur to shimmer and shine . . . with ah, bright wings!

Augustine encourages us to correct one another, with love of the person and hatred of the offense. Love for the sinner, hatred for the sin: a courageous choice! Imagine how many wars would be prevented, how many hurts avoided, how much energy better directed, if we learned how to recognize what is good in each and every person instead of demonizing, hating, and wanting to eliminate those we disagree with or who disagree and even hate us! Imagine how much better the world would be if we heeded Augustine's call instead of speaking ill of someone, wishing them to be out of our lives, and recognizing only the evil they do and not the good that is in them, even if they themselves are unwilling to recognize that good.

Fraternal correction is perhaps the least observed of the gospel mandates, and that is no little thing. Building a better world is a lifelong project—a task made more difficult for us as our attention span diminishes according to the time span between commercials—God's plan made present on its way to completion, when Christ will be all in all.

Living in harmony requires a daily effort:

- to accept one another
- to forgive one another
- to carry one another's heavy burdens willingly
- to repay evil with good

All this means working together to attain a deeper communion. One of the indispensable evangelical means to achieve this cooperation is fraternal correction (Mt 18:15-21), an instrument which Augustine makes part of his own experience of community (*Rule*, chapter 4).

What Is Fraternal Correction?

Fraternal correction is an evangelical way of relating to the sin of another. It is not an extemporaneous intervention for the purpose of restoring a lost harmony or peace. Fraternal correction is necessarily preceded by a serious process of discernment in which a brother examines his real motives for possible intervention.

In every act of fraternal correction, there must always be the element of fraternal encouragement and, indeed, the latter must be more obvious than the former. We must rely on the positive to correct the negative. The aim is to correct by encouraging and to encourage by correcting.

We are a community of saints and sinners. Day after day, we are surprised to discover that we need one another, that the holy person we carry within us is less holy if it does not learn to live with the sinner who abides within.

Augustine remarks:

> Put up with one another; if there is nothing in you which others must put up with, you will be stronger in putting up with others. If you abandon human matters and distance

yourself from the world in order that no one may see, whom can you help? And will you attain this goal without anyone's help? Charity urges us to support one another by bearing one another's burdens. When deer have to cross a river, each animal rests its head on the back of the one ahead of it. In the same way, by putting up with and helping one another, we can cross broad rivers safely and together reach the other bank. (*A Miscellany of Eighty-three Questions* 71, 1)

In this plan of holiness, there is a place not only for those who already manifest greater holiness in their life, but also for all of us, even those in whom sin or selfishness predominates. Supporting God in one another, not treating anyone as though they were utterly evil, is the challenge of following Christ in the footsteps of Augustine. As in his own life, so too for those who, in their weakness, have experienced the Father's mercy. We are all called to be merciful in turn toward the weaknesses of others. The renewal of our life in Christ can only be the fruit of a communal activity, a fraternal undertaking that methodically, and also incessantly, learns new ways of living and serving, new motivations in the relationships of communal and apostolic life. Key to all is to be able to see the butterfly in the caterpillar; to be repulsed by the sin, while yet being able to love the sinner.

Points Made by Saint Augustine Regarding Fraternal Correction:

1. The essential presupposition: charity

No one who has not overcome with love the desire for vengeance should attempt fraternal correction. In fact, if hate exists, fraternal correction is impossible, since it flows from a desire to heal, not to wound. "May your charity be enthusiastic in correcting and admonishing." (*Commentary on the first Letter of John* 7, 11)

2. The theological foundation: God corrects those whom he loves

God seeks the conversion of the sinner, not his death. It is God who corrects the one he loves. Only God is capable of combining mercy and justice. Our participation in fraternal correction needs to be inspired by divine instruction. "Look at the manner in which the Father entices us: by the allure of his teaching and not by violent imposition." (*Commentary on the Gospel of John* 26, 7)

3. The universal principle: "Love the sinner, hate the sin"

Each person is responsible for the evil he does. From this principle is derived the need for fraternal correction, and from this same principle, Augustine deduces the obligation to recognize always the good present in each person. It is from this presence of the image of God that fraternal correction flows.

> If you hear your neighbor's case in the same way as you hear your own, you will attack the sins, not the sinner. And if it happens that someone stubbornly refuses to correct his sins and has turned his back on the fear of God, then that is what you will attack in him, that is what you will try to correct, that is what you will work hard to eradicate, that the person may be preserved while the sin is condemned. There are two words here, "person" and "sinner." Man is what God created, sinner is what man made himself into. Let what man has made perish, and what God has made be set free. So do not condemn people to death, or while you are attacking the sin you will destroy the man. Do not condemn to death, and there will be someone there who can repent. Do not have a person put to death, and you will have someone who can repent. Do not have a person put to death, and you will have someone who can be reformed. As a man having

this kind of love for men in your heart, be a judge of the earth. Love terrifying them if you like, but still go on loving. If you must be high and mighty, be high and mighty against the sin, not against the person." (Sermon 13, 8)

4. *The anthropological foundation: humility*

Humility needs to be the predisposition of the person who wants to correct. Humility moves us to first recognize the beam in our own eye before trying to remove the straw from someone else's eye. Augustine encourages us to never forget that we are earthen vessels. "If, examining yourself you realize you are subject to the same defects and try to correct your brother, leave aside reproaches, cry out together with him, invite him not to obey you but rather to struggle together with you." (*Commentary on the Sermon on the Mount* 2, 19, 64)

5. *The fruit of fraternal correction: prayer*

Since fraternal correction is in God's service, prayer is natural to the one who corrects as well as to bearing fruit in the one corrected. Augustine insists that prayer alone is not enough; one must have the courage to correct. "Encourage by prayer, not by arguing; exhort in prayer, inviting cordially." (*Commentary on the Gospel of John* 6, 15)

6. *The duty of fraternal correction*

There are motives that dispense us from the obligation of fraternal correction, such as: waiting for the proper moment; reasonable doubt that the fraternal correction will be well received; fear that someone might be lost through fraternal correction; the danger of scandalizing the weak. For Augustine, fraternal correction is not an absolute obligation but rather one subject to charity and the need to maintain peace in the community. "In correcting, utilize mercy; what cannot be corrected, support with patience. For those reflecting on these things, do not reject severe discipline in order to conserve unity, nor break the bond of fraternity with exaggerated correction." (*Against Parmenian* 3, 15)

How simple it is to fall into the culturally accepted practice of thinking and speaking negatively about someone from the opposite political party, from a different race, economic, or social background! We decide to believe that God is with us, excusing even our worst traits, while condemning and imputing negative motivations on anyone we dislike or abhor, or merely disagree with.

How important it would be as a witness for our concern for our planet to not only pick up the trash, avoid littering and strewing unwanted objects in the environment, but also to avoid speaking ill of one another, thinking unkind thoughts, and spreading vicious rumors, imputing motives, belittling actions, and destroying reputations!

Integral ecology stares us in the face in this chapter, seeking our ongoing conversion and stable growth. By identifying nature as one of the important dynamic levels of relationships, along with love of God, others, and self, we can follow Augustine's path to conversion, from self-centeredness to appreciating the goodness in all that surrounds us, meanwhile promoting greater communion and living more harmoniously.

Integral ecology urges us to be attentive to the cry of both the planet and the poor, to bear the burden, to give the benefit of the doubt, to believe in one another, to give yet another chance, seventy times seven.

Jesus loved Judas, as hard as that may seem to us; he prayed for him, washed his feet, and served him at the table, just as he did Peter. Jesus forgave those who blasphemed, cursed, betrayed, gave false testimony, and nailed him to the cross. Jesus' response was not to seek vengeance, not to eliminate those who hated him, but to eliminate hate from his own heart, longing and acting so as to conquer the hate in the hearts of others.

Who have I belittled today, to whom have I imputed motives, trashed their reputation? What politician, neighbor, fellow worker, family member is the butt of my jokes, the object of my hatred, unworthy of my compassion?

Augustine encourages us in this chapter: God who dwells within you will protect you from within yourself. As we attempt to live more simply, *Laudato si'* invites us to follow the "little way of Saint Thérèse of Lisieux." As for her, so too for us, an integral ecology is made up of daily gestures which break the logic of violence, exploitation, and selfishness. In the end, a world of exacerbated consumption is at the same time a world that mistreats life in all its forms.

In *The City of God* (XV, 5), Augustine reminds us: The possession of goodness is by no means diminished by being shared; on the contrary, it is increased in proportion to the concord and charity of each of those who share it.

God cares for us when we are cared for by another, in love. One clear manifestation of such care is the obligation to speak fraternally to another who is in danger of harming themselves or the community by their actions. Ultimately, such admonishment must always manifest the tender mercy and forgiveness of God. When in need of assistance, we must graciously accept the help given. We must humbly accept fraternal correction, which is based on truth and offered in a charitable spirit, which we believe helps build each other up.

I encourage you to take the time to examine your relationships. Perhaps the following guide might help you:

- In whom do I find it difficult or am unable to see and appreciate God's presence?
- Am I willing to step back from initial distaste and even spontaneous dislike or hatred in order to discover something of good, of God, in any and everybody?
- Am I treating any one or any group of people as objects, there for my satisfaction, without taking into account their needs and wants?
- Do I greet the person who serves my food and thank the person at the cash register? Do I wish the person who drives the bus a good day?
- Whom do I pray for? Just for my needs, or in gratitude to God for placing other people and things in my path?

- What's the next possible step I can take toward improving my relationships?
- Who is waiting for me for fraternal correction (for me or from me)?

Conscious that relationships are always in a state of flux, we seek God's help to be able to take the next possible step toward a better world for all.

God of all, may we be moved to tap into the countless ways that human ingenuity, animated by your Spirit, has allowed us to collectively live more sustainably on the Earth, protecting the dignity of people and planet.

We pray that we always prioritize the dignity and rights of workers as we make purchasing decisions in our families and communities, and that we consider how our financial investments impact the health of the planet.

Help us to become more aware of our mutual responsibility for growing in communion.

Serving the Greater Good Through the Communion of Goods

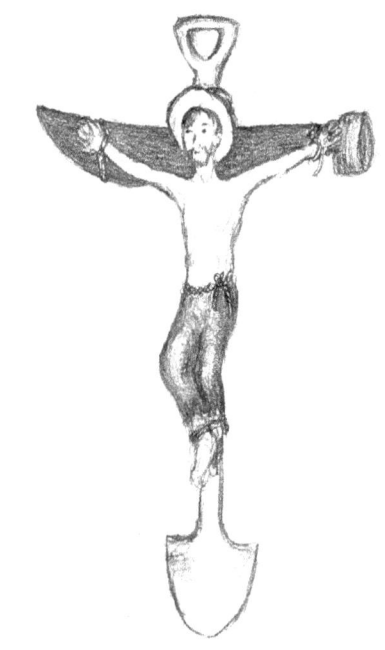

Another Vignette to Introduce Us to the Call to Conversion

When I think about the principle of solidarity, my mind and heart conjure up the person of Max Inga. Let me share with you why.

Max lived with his family in the farming community located about five miles outside of Chulucanas, Peru, just on the other side of the mostly empty riverbed, since that portion of the Sechura Desert rarely saw rain. When rain did come, in the month of March (an extremely short rainy "season"), the river would flow and leave deep in its bed the remarkable product we know as clay. The town was called La Encantada, the enchanted village.

In the late 1960s, when Chulucanas had no hospital and the only medical attention was provided by Marist Missionary Sisters at a small clinic, Max was thirteen years old, and his limbs were beginning to lose strength.

Sister Gloria Joyce did the tests and told Max and his family that he had multiple sclerosis and would slowly lose the use of his limbs. Max was distraught, saying, "I am a poor campesino; my family lives from farming; how am I going to survive?"

Sister Gloria, trying to encourage Max, told him that there are many other ways to make a living besides farming. Max questioned her: "What else could I do?" Sister told him he could make straw sombreros, pottery, and other similar tasks. None impressed Max, but he said, "Well, who would teach me?" Never one to get caught without something to say, Sister Gloria told him that she would. So, Max decided on ceramics, which was an unknown profession in Chulucanas at that time.

Sister Gloria got a good book and studied up on the topic. She got a few other students of a similar age to accompany Max and began what proved to be an unbelievable journey.

Max and two other students became so adept that they began to win regional, then national, prizes. One of Max's first creations was a crucifix made of a shovel and a machete, the tools of the local farmers, on which hung the figure of Christ dressed as a typical local farmer, with a sombrero and a rope as a belt to hold up his raggedy pants.

Max would tell those who asked that this is how he saw the suffering Christ present in his people today, crucified on the instruments of their labor, farming in an area dominated by the second driest desert in the world.

Max traveled to Washington, D.C., as well as Paris, for an exhibition of his work. Several professionals encouraged Max to stay in the United States to get better attention for his illness.

Max chose to continue to live in the village where he was born, in the same adobe hut in which he was born. Instead of getting ahead by himself, he dedicated himself to teaching other special needs children the art of ceramics, and then their entire family as well.

Today, La Encantada—a truly enchanted village—has 120 families who live from producing ceramics, a great tribute to Max's commitment to his people. Chulucanas is known internationally for its ceramics.

Max eventually married, had three children of his own (all girls), and then adopted a baby boy shortly before the disease he had lived with took his breath away. But it was unable to take from his heart the firm commitment to share with others what God had shared with him.

For me, and for many others, Max personifies solidarity.

The Rule of Augustine, Chapter 5

30. Your clothes should be looked after in common by one or more brothers who are to see that they are well aired and kept free from moths. Just as the food you eat is prepared in the one kitchen, so the clothes you wear are to come from the one storeroom.

    And as far as possible, it should not matter to you greatly which summer or winter clothes you receive. It does not make any difference whether you get back the same clothes you handed in or something that has been worn by another, "provided no one is denied what he needs." If this gives rise to jealousy or grumbling, or if people begin complaining that the clothes they now have are not as good as those they had before, or if they think it beneath them to wear clothes that had previously been worn by others, does that not tell you something? If the external matter of dress becomes a cause of discord, does this not prove that inwardly, in the attitude of your heart, there is something sadly lacking? But if you are unable to do these things and your weakness is taken into consideration so that you are allowed to receive again the same clothes you handed in, even so, keep them all in the one place where they will be looked after by those charged with this task.

31. The intention behind all this is that no one will seek his own advantage in his work. Everything you do is to be for the service of the community, and you are to work with more zeal and enthusiasm than if each person were merely working for himself and his own interests. For it is written of love that "it is not self-seeking"; that is to say, love puts the interests of the community before personal advantage, and not the other way around. Therefore, the degree to which you are concerned for the interests of the community rather than your own, is the criterion by which you can judge how much progress you have made. Thus, in all the fleeting necessities of human life, "something sublime and permanent" reveals itself, "namely love."

32. It follows from this that a religious who receives clothes or other useful items from his parents or relatives may not keep these quietly for himself. He should place them at the disposal of the superior. "Once they have become the property of the community, it is up to the superior to see that these articles find their way into the hands of those who need them." But should anyone conceal a gift he has received, he shall be judged guilty of theft.

33. When you want to wash your clothes or have them washed at a laundry, let this take place in consultation with the superior, lest desire for clean clothes sully your character.

34. Because bathing may be necessary for good health, the opportunity to visit the public baths may never be refused. In this matter, follow medical advice without grumbling. Even if a person is unwilling, he shall do what has to be done for the good of his health, if necessary at the command of the superior. But if someone wants to go bathing just because he enjoys it when it is not really necessary, he will have to learn to renounce his desires. For what a person likes may not always be good for him. It may even be harmful.

35. In any case, if a brother says that he does not feel well, even though he is not noticeably sick, believe him without hesitation. But if you are not sure whether the treatment he wishes to have will be of any benefit to him, then consult a doctor about it.

36. See to it that there are always two or more of you when you visit the public baths. Indeed, this applies wherever you go. And it is not for you to choose the people who will go with you—you are to leave this to the decision of the superior.

37. Someone should be deputed by the community to care for the sick. At the same time the person ought to take care of those who are convalescing and those who are weak, even though they are not running a temperature. The infirmarian may take from the kitchen whatever he himself considers necessary.

38. Those responsible for food, clothes, and books should serve their brothers without grumbling.

39. Books will be available every day at the appointed hour, and not at any other time.

40. The brothers in charge of clothes and shoes should not delay in making these available to those who need them.

―――·····―――

Augustine advises us in this chapter of *The Rule* that caring for food, clothes, and books is a way of showing our concern for one another, our health, and the well-being of all, the present and future inhabitants of our planet. We are all meant to experience life in abundance, to live in harmony.

This is the most concrete portion of the *Rule* Augustine left us, the most directly involved in the intricacies of daily life together. As much as the details are time-conditioned, the underlying principles continue to be applicable in our life today.

If the very concept of public baths is no longer common nor seen as medicinal, nor the idea that only the wealthy or cultivated could afford a daily warm bath for their own pleasure, those who followed *The Rule* then (and now) are invited to opt for not aligning themselves with the wealthy but rather with the poor, who need to work and do not have the leisure time to indulge in those exquisite pleasures.

In these details, we can discern an element of social protest which would not be unwelcome in our own time: a social statement against luxury and accumulated wealth, against the idleness of the privileged. The choice remains present today: a Broadway play with its accompanying frills of dining and means of transport, or sharing a holiday meal with families restrained by soup kitchen options.

In Augustine's time, books were a very precious possession, as each volume needed to be handwritten and represented a considerable investment of time and money. The special care Augustine recommends for books can be compared with the amount of care we display for the precious gift of food or water, ever more scarce and costly, yet wasted so readily and thoughtlessly by many who seem to not consider the virtual water invested in a single hamburger, the scandal of maintaining enormous lawns for decoration, or not even contemplating the possibility of carpooling rather than the convenience of driving alone. There was a time, not long ago, when it was ordinary to share a car among the various members of a community or a family, and there has never been so much need for storage space as in our own day and age.

As Augustine suggests in *The Rule*, one concrete manner of becoming less consumer-oriented is to appreciate and care for the things we already have. This can be a first step in diminishing the growing tendency to purchase more.

In fact, the way we demonstrate our concern for providing food and clothing for each of the members of our family or community has changed dramatically.

Wages or income are called to be kept in common by *The Rule*—even when Judas's progenies continue to control the common purse. Sharing in common need not discourage personal responsibility. The recommendation Augustine makes regarding the care of common goods—of articles belonging to the community (dishwasher, lawn mower . . .)—to care for them with greater attention than things meant for our own personal use, is still quite relevant and challenging.

This chapter contains many details regarding the spirit and mentality that animate particular acts of caring for one another as loving expressions of a much deeper reality, which is directly concerned with the spirituality of communion, the ability to live in harmony with all people and things.

Envy and dissension frequently arise, now as then, in connection with material goods, as is the need for demonstrating greater concern for the good of others over my own.

"Everything you do is to be for the service of the community" can be taken as the fundamental inspiration behind the concrete recommendations given. The whole emphasis in this chapter is on looking after the material and physical well-being of others, those with whom we live, the broader community, those near and far who live in want and misery, and those generations to come.

"Thus, in all the fleeting necessities of human life something sublime and permanent reveals itself, namely love." (*Rule, chapter* 5; 31).

Sixteen centuries ago, Augustine, while contemplating how Jesus of Nazareth made the connection between solidarity and charity shine brightly before all, preached to the parish community gathered in Hippo:

> Do you think it is a small matter that you are eating someone else's food? We brought nothing into this world; you have found a full table spread for you. God bestows the world on the poor; he bestows it on the rich. (Sermon 29, 2)

Hunger and waste still exist in our day as in the early fifth century. In every part of the world, stark inequalities persist between developed and developing countries, inequalities stoked also by various forms of exploitation, oppression, and corruption that have a negative influence on the internal and international life of many countries.

Solidarity or voluntary poverty is the path leading from the inhuman condition of material poverty toward a broader experience of spiritual poverty, understood as a profound reliance on God's providence. We have been called to share generously what God has shared freely with us. We are also advised by Augustine not to be indifferent or passive in the face of misery and want.

In this regard, Pope Francis appeals to us in *Laudato si'*:

> One expression of this attitude is when we stop and give thanks to God before and after meals. I ask all believers to return to this beautiful and meaningful custom. That moment of blessing, however brief, reminds us of our dependence on God for life; it strengthens our feeling of gratitude for the gifts of creation; it acknowledges those who by their labors provide us with these goods; and it reaffirms our solidarity with those in greatest need. (no. 227)

Solidarity is not a feeling of vague compassion or shallow distress at the misfortunes of so many people, both near and far. On the contrary, it is a firm and persevering determination to commit oneself to the common good, the good of all, because we are all really responsible for all. Pope Francis said it so clearly in *On Care for Our Common Home*: Everything is interconnected, and this invites us to develop a spirituality of that global solidarity which flows from the mystery of the Trinity (no. 240).

As the *Compendium of the Social Doctrine of the Church* reminds us:

> The principle of solidarity requires that men and women of our day cultivate a greater awareness that they are debtors of the society of which they have become part. A similar debt must be recognized in the various forms of social interaction, so that humanity's journey will not be interrupted but remain open to present and future generations, all of them called together to share the same gift in solidarity. (no. 195)

The "structures of sin" that dominate relationships between people and nations must be overcome based on the principle of solidarity. They must be transformed into structures of solidarity through the conversion of lifestyles and the identification of guidelines and directives that help promote this new lifestyle.

We acknowledge that the economy is a sub-system of human society, which itself is embedded within our common home. A commitment to live the principle of solidarity provides us with the challenge of putting the economy at the service of the people and not the people at the service of the economy.

The central idea of this chapter can be summed up in the principle of solidarity: Therefore, the degree to which you can be concerned for the interests of the community rather than for your own is the criterion by which you can judge how much progress you have made.

Augustine contends that there is no possibility of genuine community of mind and heart without the virtue of humility. It is the primary virtue for common life. Conversely, pride, which lurks even in good works, is the beginning and origin of all sin. It is misguided self-love, attributing to ourselves the good intentions and admirable actions, when their actual origin is the God who resides within us.

Just as Christ emptied himself, so too do we need to guard against pride, which can undermine a good work and distort both origin and motivation. Social status, education, possessions, and high achievements do not make us who we are, except when pride dominates. The incarnation of the Word of God is witnessed to in the practice of humility. When we imitate Christ in practicing humility, we are formed in his image by loving God and others more than self. We depend on God for all that we are and what we have.

Charity grows whenever the individual or the community freely choose to place the greater good ahead of their own. We are called to build the reign of God, not our own sandcastle. Cooperation, collaboration, and the recognition of the gifts of others enhance the growth of community. The measure of our growth in charity is found in our placing the interest of the community before our own.

Augustine, in the later books of his *Confessions*, following the narration of his conversion experience in the garden, delved deeply into the study of creation as described in Genesis, expanding his understanding of God, the Trinity, time, and the relationship between heaven and earth. In those chapters, the gift of creation is attributed by Augustine to God's love for us, positioning creation at the center of a loving relationship desired by God.

So too, when we unshackle ourselves from excessive consumerism and the endless accumulation of material goods that obscures our vision and makes it difficult to discover and contemplate God present in nature and in everything around us, we will have the opportunity to experience the interconnectedness with all of creation that Augustine expresses so clearly.

> Observe the beauty of the world and praise the plan of the creator. Observe what he made, love the one who made it. Hold on to this maxim above all: love the one who made it, because he also made you, his lover, in his own image. (Sermon 68, 5)

> In Sermon 68, Augustine reminds us that to find God, "We can read a book, a certain great big book, the book of created nature." The wonder and awe we experience are expressions of worship and gratitude to the God who made all this for us to enjoy—not, however, at the expense of the dignity of others.

Concretely, let's examine our relationship with food, the staff of life, the most precious thing we hold in common. Caring for food is equivalent to treasuring life. The world produces more than enough food for everyone, yet a billion people are hungry, and an equivalent amount are overweight or obese. Both groups are devastatingly poor and are being failed by societal structures.

Food is our closest connection to nature—God's gift to all but managed to the benefit of a small segment. If we are all guests at the same table, it seems appropriate to ask, Who is hosting the meal, inviting, seating, and distributing the bounty? Food is the source from which we and our society grows; it is rooted in every level of our lives, of unequaled influence in our world.

Here are some questions related to integral ecology, inspired by this chapter of *The Rule* that we might ask ourselves:

- The distance of "food miles"—referring to the distance food travels from where it grows to where it is consumed—has been steadily increasing over the past fifty years. Fruits and vegetables travel an average of 1,500 miles from the farm to our table. Can we plan to investigate the food miles of our regularly purchased fruits and vegetables to perhaps consider other possibilities?

- How do the ways we invest or spend our money demonstrate our concern for the environment, our commitment to workers, and to the people most vulnerable to the harm of climate change and environmental degradation?

- Examine any product you are thinking of purchasing and ask yourself these questions:

  - Is the item a want or a need? Is it truly vital to your well-being and happiness?
  - What are the effects, both positive and negative, on you, on other people, animals, and the environment?
  - What systems support, promote, and perpetuate this item?
  - What would be an alternative that would do more good and less harm?

The true-price exercise encourages us to examine more deeply and critically, not only the impacts, but also our own beliefs and assumptions about what we think we know.

Forgiving One Another

*Who injures the name of an absent friend
may not at this table as guest attend*

Carved into the table of the dining room of Augustine's community in Hippo

A Vignette to Situate the Topic of This Chapter

María Elena Moyano (November 29, 1958 to February 15, 1992) was a community organizer and activist of Afro-Peruvian origin, a daughter, a sister, a wife, and a mother. She was assassinated by the Maoist Shining Path (Sendero Luminoso) insurgent movement.

María Elena was born in Lima, and she began her community involvement during her teens in a youth movement in Villa El

Salvador, a vast shantytown on the outskirts of the capital, largely populated by migrants from the interior of the country.

When she was twenty-four, she was elected president of the federation of women from Villa El Salvador. Under her leadership, the movement grew to encompass public kitchens, health committees, and a program which supplied children with milk each day. She was later elected deputy mayor of the municipality of Villa El Salvador.

At this time, the Shining Path guerillas were trying to consolidate their hold on the poorer neighborhoods of Lima. They sought to undermine the Peruvian government in order to assume control of the country. They killed more than thirty thousand people, instilling fear and insecurity.

María Elena confronted the Shining Path guerillas, calling them terrorists, not revolutionaries. She became known as Mother Courage for her willingness to stand up in the face of death threats. She led a protest march against the Shining Path in which people carried white banners as a symbol of peace. After the protest, she was gunned down at a fundraising meal for a group of women, her body dynamited in front of her husband and children.

More than three hundred thousand people attended her funeral as a sign of hope and defiance. At her funeral, Gustavo Gutiérrez declared: "Those who blew María Elena's body to pieces, wanting to make it disappear, have only managed to spread more of the seeds of life that will germinate very soon."

María Elena Moyano: Mother Courage, in the face of the violence of Sendero Luminoso, lived her life to the full, serving and sharing, relying utterly on God.

The Rule of Augustine, Chapter 6

41. Do not quarrel. But if you do have a quarrel, put an end to it as quickly as possible. Otherwise, an isolated moment of anger grows into hatred, "the splinter becomes a beam," and you make your heart a murderer's den. For we read in the Scriptures: "Whoever hates his brother is a murderer."

42. If you have hurt a person by abusing him, or by cursing or grossly accusing him, be careful to make amends for the harm you have done, as quickly as possible, by apologizing to him. And the one who has been hurt should be ready in his turn to forgive you without wrangling. Brothers who have insulted each other should "forgive each other's trespasses." If you fail to do this, your praying the Our Father becomes a lie. Indeed, the more you pray, the more honest your prayer ought to become.

    It is better to have to deal with a person who, though quick to anger, immediately seeks a reconciliation once he realizes he has been unjust to another, than with someone who is less easily roused, but also less inclined to seek forgiveness. But "a person who never wants to ask forgiveness, or who fails to do so from the heart," does not belong in the religious community, even though he may not be sent away.

    Be cautious of hard words. Should you utter them, then do not be afraid to speak the healing word with the same mouth that caused the wound.

43. From time to time, the necessity of keeping order may compel you to use harsh words to the young people who have not yet reached adulthood, in order to keep them in line. In that case, you are not required to apologize, even though you yourself consider that you have gone too far. For if you are too humble and submissive in your conduct toward these young people, then your authority, which they should be ready to accept, will be undermined. In such cases, you should ask the forgiveness from the Lord of all, who knows with what deep affection you love your brothers, even those you might happen to have reproved with undue severity. Do not let love for one another remain caught up in self-love; rather, such love must be guided by the Spirit.

Living in harmony seems so innocuous, utterly harmless, and inoffensive. Of course, who would not want to live in peaceful accord, appreciating divergent opinions, and encouraging frank statements of opinion.

Augustine wrote quite attractively of friendship in the *Confessions*, sharing the lived experience of harmony:

> My greatest comfort and relief is in the consolation of friends. Friendship has joys that captivate my heart—the charms of talking and laughing together and kindly giving way to each other's wishes, reading elegantly written books together, sharing jokes and delighting to honor one another. If we disagree with each other occasionally, it is without malice, as a person might disagree with himself, and the rare occasions of dispute lend spice to season our much more frequent accord. We teach and learn from each other, sadly missing any who are absent and gladly welcoming them when they come home. Such signs of friendship spring from the hearts of friends who love and know they are loved in return, signs to be read in smiles, words, glances and a thousand gracious gestures. These are sparks that kindle a blaze to melt our hearts and fuse them inseparably into one." (*Confessions*, IV, viii, 13)

As attractive as this description seems, we all understand that it merely captures one frame in a moving picture. Our lives are not a series of set pieces but rather ongoing dynamic processes, actions, and reactions. Relationships, like the flame pictured above the heart which Augustine holds in his hand, stir up and die down in an endless progression. What we observe regarding human relationships finds easy comparison in the rest of creation as well.

A community of life without conflict is impossible. Living together and interacting is bound to create conflicts, and Augustine, in *The Rule*, offers us a way to respond to these situations. Disputes are to be addressed quickly, directly, and with compassion. The one who has been offended must be ready to forgive. Authentic forgiveness comes from the heart, not just the lips. To forgive from the heart requires humility, as Augustine stated when commenting earlier in *The Rule* on the impossibility of communion of mind and heart without this essential virtue.

Harmony is both a gift and a task. To the extent that we actively participate harmoniously in life with God, the God-as-communion becomes more present in and among us, enabling us to live in harmony.

Sometimes we expect that the gift of harmony will bear fruit among us without much personal investment on our part. On the other hand, we must attend to the fact that the task of building a community is a process and not something either immediately produced, automatic, or permanent.

We very often want the gift of a harmonious life, but without accepting the task that the building of communion entails. Dialogue is critical to this process.

Dialogue implies placing yourself in the presence of others on an equal footing, not because we all have the same talents or gifts, but rather because we all share the same dignity. No one has more dignity, no one has less; we are all created in the image and likeness of God, and from this flows our dignity.

For a successful dialogue aimed at achieving a greater communion, it is necessary that each one recognize the other to be a person endowed by God with personal dignity, with a conscience and freedom, and with the possibility of growth. At the Last Supper, Jesus gave expression to his deepest desire at that very important moment: unity modeled on the Trinity:

> That they may all be one. As you, Father, are in me and I am in you, may they also be in us, so that the world may believe that you have sent me. The glory that you have given me I have given them, so that they may be one, as we are one, I in them and you in me, that they may become completely one, so that the world may know that you have sent me and have loved them even as you have loved me. (Jn 17:21-23)

If we ask, "Why carry on dialogue?" the answer is not so much that we may reach agreement or communicate information but rather that we may journey toward the unity Christ so greatly desired: a unity of mind and heart. The way in which we place ourselves in relationship to others can allow us to grow and achieve a deeper communion and live more fully the unity modeled for us by the Trinity. Our *Rule* urges us to "live together in oneness of mind and heart, mutually honoring God in yourselves, whose temples you have become" (chapter 1, no. 8).

One Mind

This means being united in our search for truth; it means progressively drawing closer in a reciprocal enrichment of ideas toward a profound agreement with those we love. It requires giving and receiving: Each person creates a space that allows others to contribute, from their point of view, to a fuller understanding of the truth. No one regards his opinion as wholly formed and fixed, once and for all, but rather as always open to the views of others.

One Heart

This means unity in desire and in action. This unity is one of wills (concord), which precedes and accompanies every genuine dialogue. It calls for "benevolence" (desiring the good of others, thinking well of others, speaking well of others, and doing good to and for others), which in turn promotes trust. It demands that one's supreme desire be to seek not one's own personal good but rather the common good.

The journey toward harmonious living follows the gentle path of genuine dialogue. It is through dialogue that a community achieves a greater unity and a deeper harmony in ideals. This journey requires constant growth and conversion, dying and rising in true humility.

Augustine makes it eminently clear that a community will be strong only if its members interact honestly and lovingly. Reconciliation is based on true concern for each other's welfare. Open, forthright, and loving confrontation is required to point out what is truly harmful to one another and to the community for the welfare of all.

Our commitment to live harmoniously depends on developing a truly integral ecology: caring about the whole person and all people, considering all levels of our relationships, with ourselves, others, God, and nature, in order to avoid imbalance, skewing, and dissonance.

We are familiar with the scriptural phrase repeated often at worship, recognizing that only God is truly holy: "Holy, Holy, Holy, Lord God of hosts, heaven and earth are filled with your glory."

All creation is invited to manifest the holiness of God; all, too, are tempted by the desire to possess what we admire. God's holiness is freely shared with us, without conditions and without limits. When we claim to possess the holiness of God, we reveal how little we truly understand God and ourselves.

As Benedict XVI preached on assuming the papacy: "The external deserts in the world are growing, because the internal deserts have become so vast."

Something within us simply misleads us, triggering the belief that we can save someone else, and we can bring God to those who don't know God. We truly do not know God if we think that God is not already present: heaven and earth are filled with your glory!

At best, we can discover God in ourselves and others, and help others, perhaps, to recognize or discover God in themselves, in their best intentions, to go out of themselves in order to enter into communion with others. Conflict arises when we want to save someone else, when we want them to be who we think they should be. We want to be considered their savior or messiah.

María Elena Moyano is an example of someone who faced life-threatening conflict with outstanding courage, even to the extent of losing her life, and who was willing to risk all in order to provide hope and relief for so many needy families. Her life, given in service to others, gives witness to the conflict of interests in our world. Selfishness versus selflessness, pride versus humility.

Conflict management and conflict resolution are skills that can bring us all closer to living in harmony, but even the grace of God allows itself to be bound by our selfishness. To impose rather than invite or propose, to choose the path of authoritarian control as opposed to reasonable dialogue, have not been able to dim the light which emanates from the empty tomb of our risen Lord and Savior.

We certainly have no reason to believe that the community that gathered around Jesus during his public ministry did not have its difficulties and conflicts. Clearly, there existed tension in that community, conflicts perhaps much deeper than those we may experience in our local community.

Life without tension can best be found while visiting the graveyard, alone. Relationships are work and they tend to be imperfect by nature, causing tension and some level of conflict. The way in which we handle conflicts defines us as Christians. It is not possible to be a Christian only in the chapel or the apostolate but not in the house with the community, with our family.

A community is comprised not of uniform members but of diverse people united in mind and heart, each sharing from their own identity and being enriched by the gifts of others. Harmony cannot happen without diversity or variety.

Conflict is usually thought of as something negative: It makes us think of opposed and mutually exclusive positions, of controversy, of disagreement. But conflict is in itself neither negative nor positive. Its significance depends on how it is handled.

In this chapter, Augustine offers guidance on how to bear with one another, offering advice on how to act when faced with the inevitable conflicts:

- Settle quarrels or conflicts swiftly; it's better to prevent quarrels than to have to remedy their results.

- Avoid exaggerating the faults of others while ignoring our own; it's so easy to make excuses or diminish the importance when faced with our own foibles, or those of the ones we love, while amplifying those of others whom we appreciate less.

- Dishonesty and hypocrisy occur when we consider ourselves better or worse than others; in truth, we are all different (thank God!), and we need one another's gifts and talents to become all that we can be for others.

- Hatred leads to death, my own as well as that of others; hatred, for Augustine, is the exact opposite of love. It is malevolence as opposed to benevolence, and it results in killing myself since hatred is death more radical than that of the body; by hatred, the soul itself is destroyed.
- Ask for pardon as soon as possible; this is frequently more difficult than actually pardoning.
- Be ready to forgive without wrangling; closing ourselves to another is closing ourselves to God.

In our process of conversion toward an integral ecology, it would be healthy and wise to think of how this guidance might be applicable not only to us personally but also to us as a people, and in relation to our environment as well.

Augustine says: "Let us teach, with as much insistence as we can, our dearest friends who sincerely foster our labors, that they may know that it is possible that among friends one contradicts the words of another, though love is, nonetheless, not diminished and though the truth, which is owed to friendship, does not give birth to hatred" (Letter I, 82).

For example, *The Rule* invites us "to forgive one another their guilt because of our prayers": We might consider how retribution remains impending in regard to racism and exploitation of people as well as terrain.

Another Vignette Might Help Grasp the Significance of Forgiving from the Heart

Forgiveness seems so far beyond our power at times, and it truly is. The source of forgiveness comes from beyond us. It is divine: our loving and compassionate God.

A father of a big family had a job working in Center City, Philadelphia. One night, he left work very late when, suddenly, someone tried to grab his briefcase from behind. He pulled it back and could see that the mugger trying to steal the briefcase was high on drugs and had a gun. The mugger shot and pistol-whipped the man and left him to die, unconscious and bleeding on the sidewalk. Fortunately, a driver stopped and called for help. An ambulance took him to a local hospital, where his life was saved.

At some point in the medical process, the hospital provided counseling to deal with the trauma and possible anger issues caused by the attack. The counselor asked if the man was angry at his assailant. He paused and said, "Not angry. In fact, I forgive him, but it makes me sad that one person could inflict such pain on another." He forgave the man but hated the desperation the assailant was driven to by his need for money to feed a drug habit.

From what wellspring spouts the ability of the victim to forgive the perpetrator? So often, too often, the physical damage done to the victim is exacerbated by internalizing anger and hatred, which—if allowed to grow—will eat away, corroding and destroying the ability to enjoy life to the full. If the victim can open their mind and heart to feel for the perpetrator, and recognize their wounded humanity enough to be saddened by their condition, our ability to grow through tragedy abounds.

On a heroic level, we can call to mind Pope Saint John Paul II, who forgave the person who tried to assassinate him in Saint Peter's Square. We can almost expect that of someone who is pope. But there are many who are not outstandingly religious men or women, who also courageously open themselves up to new horizons by truly forgiving the wrongdoer. Their witness allows us to believe in the God who empties himself for love of us.

In a sermon addressed to the people of Hippo, sixteen centuries ago, and to us today, Augustine advises how our praying the Our Father can easily become a lie:

> Let us then daily—and with true heart—say: "Forgive us our trespasses as we forgive those who trespass against us." And, moreover, let us do what we say. We enter a bond with God, an agreement, an engagement. (Sermon 56, 9)

But if we do not in fact forgive the debt, we are not keeping our agreement with God; we are breaking that bond. The decision to forgive is not a natural reaction but a divine choice, a willing participation in the life of Christ. Forgiveness of those who do us harm is at the heart of being a Christian (Mt 5:23-24).

To decide not to forgive is to condemn oneself to a fruitless and destructive repetition of evil, a stagnant and unproductive personal and communal life, obsessed with the hurts of the past.

The proof of forgiveness is not forgetfulness of the past but the healing of the wound. Painful memories never disappear entirely. The real task is not to allow these memories to control the way we act in the present. To hold on to these feelings makes it difficult for the person and the community to grow. Forgiveness brings peace not only to the one who has offended but also to the one who forgives.

Forgiveness sets the person free and offers hope of a new life. When our emotional state depends on the memory of hurts we have suffered, we are allowing the person who offended us to continue to control our life. Forgiveness frees the victim from the control of the one who caused the pain.

Forgiveness is beneficial to one's emotional health. Anger is a very painful emotion and can even destroy the person who allows it to simmer within himself. Forgiveness is beneficial to bodily health. Anger causes physical problems such as ulcers, strokes, and bleeding.

Forgiveness helps us to live fully in the present. We condemn ourselves to live in the past if our lives are focused on vengeance and calling to mind, ceaselessly, offenses suffered in the past.

The decision to forgive an offender is a difficult one. We can choose either to hold on to the grievance or to let it go. One of the greatest obstacles to the building of community is the decision of its members not to forgive past offenses.

Think of how we can apply this learning to environmental restoration where pollution and contamination have damaged whole neighborhoods, disproportionately increasing the incidence of major diseases among those who are most poor.

We can think of waste prevention as opposed to waste disposal (by burying or burning). The land, animals, plants, and the atmosphere itself await our contribution toward restoration, our commitment to redress the debt we have accrued to future generations.

Building a community involves forbearance and forgiveness, avoiding quarrels, and repairing quickly the damage done. But there are many other pathways, which this chapter invites us to consider, for building community, for contributing to making this world a better place for all.

Harmonious living doesn't simply happen; we are invited to be co-creators of a better world for all. Building community begins at home, with you and me:

- Walk around your neighborhood.
- Greet your neighbors.
- Sit on the stoop.
- Plant flowers.
- Use the local library.
- Buy from local merchants.
- Share a plant or flowers with neighbors.
- Take a walk in the park.
- Pick up litter.
- Offer to carry the neighbor's groceries.
- Hire young people for odd jobs.
- Bake extra and share.
- Ask for help when you need it.
- Seek to understand by asking questions and listening to the answers.

Responsible Authority Through Listening and Love

Another Vignette to Help Situate the Topic of This Chapter

Martín was a poor, Black boy with an absent father, in a country where the law prohibited descendants of the African slaves from becoming professed members of religious orders. He was the illegitimate son of a Spanish nobleman—who abandoned Martín and his Black mother—possibly a freed slave—Ana Velásquez.

Martín de Porres was born in Lima, Peru, in 1579, into the kind of poverty familiar to many of the world's children even now. How easy it would have been for him to allow resentment and anger to grow in his heart. Instead, he learned to cultivate the love of Christ and to love others as Christ did.

The boy learned to cut hair and tend the sick, which became tools for him to serve his neighbor in humility, after the example of the master footwasher. Desiring to be surrounded by others who loved Christ, he asked to be accepted by the Dominican priory in Lima as a lay helper.

Among the Dominican friars, some were hard-hearted. "Mulatto dog," some called him; yet another mocked him for his illegitimate birth. While Martín suffered these taunts, they did not disturb his peace. He was God's servant and the servant of his brothers, even if they were cruel.

For eight years, he dedicated himself to the humblest service, cutting the friars' hair, scrubbing, sweeping, and attending the door, which involved attending to the needs of the poor who came knocking. His humble witness won him approval to be admitted as a professed brother despite the law, which would not allow this young mulatto to take vows. The Dominicans follow *The Rule of Augustine* as their foundational guide.

Martín was accepted into the community and placed in charge of the infirmary. He cared for the sick friars, but also for others, noblemen and slaves. People felt the love in him. Many of the friars came to see the depths of charity and prayer in this young mixed-race man who was their brother.

Martín begged for alms in the nearby market and was able to feed 160 poor people each day, while also distributing an astonishing sum of money every week to the indigent. Side by side with his daily work in the kitchen, laundry, and infirmary, Martín founded a residence for orphans and abandoned children in the city of Lima.

When Martín died, at the age of fifty-nine, his fellow friars and many in the city already knew that this "poor mulatto" who served the poor because he was one of them, this simple friar who humbled the proud, was their brother, and a true saint.

Martín de Porres was the victim of prejudice due to his race and economic condition. Even as a religious, he was relegated to places considered inferior, serving as a porter in the doorway, miraculously transforming it into a privileged place for caring and sharing from his poverty. He dedicated time to begging from merchants and customers to share with those most in need. He was humble but definitely not humiliated into passivity, nor reactionary violence, always at the service of the reign of God, a promoter of communion, a builder of community, who lived in harmony with God, self, others, and nature.

The Rule of Augustine, Chapter 7

44. "Obey your superior" as a father, but also give him due respect on account of his office; otherwise, you offend God in him. This is even more true [of] the priest who bears responsibility for you all.

45. It is primarily up to the superior to see that all that has been said here is put into practice and that infringements are not carelessly overlooked. It is his duty to point out the abuses and to correct them. If something is beyond his competence and power, he should put the matter before the priest, whose authority in some respects is greater than his own.

46. Your superior must not think himself fortunate in "having power to lord it over you," but in "the love with which he will serve you." Because of your esteem for him, he shall be superior to you; because of his responsibility to God, he shall realize that he is the very least of all the brethren. "Let him show himself an example to all in good work; he is to reprimand those who neglect their work, to give courage to those who are disheartened, to support the weak, and to be patient with everyone." He should himself observe the norms of the community and so lead others to respect them too. And let him strive to be loved by you rather than to be feared, although both love and respect are necessary. He should remember that "he is responsible to God for you."

47. By your ready and loving obedience, therefore, you not only "show compassion to yourselves," but also to your superior. For it applies to you as well that the higher the position a person holds, the greater the danger he is in.

Responsible Authority Through Listening and Love

In this chapter of *The Rule*, Augustine speaks to us of authority and service; we can learn much about both of these from the life and example of Saint Martín de Porres. Without a doubt, this involves becoming more aware of the current situation of those who suffer due to prejudice and exclusion, as well as the willingness to make a firm commitment to move forward toward the ideal for which we strive, recalling that the fruit is already present in the seed, emphasizing the need to be the change we hope for.

Did Martín lend his life to help build a better world for all? Without a doubt. But the task is ongoing, calling for renewed commitment to overcome the tug toward individualism and accumulation of material possessions. Some would recommend imposing laws and reforming structures. Martín, along with Christ, chose the path of humble service, building up community day by day.

Saint Martín is often depicted holding a broom, symbolizing his humble service and willingness to perform menial tasks. His life and actions highlight the importance of humility, compassion, and selfless service, which are all themes central to the Gospel story of Jesus washing feet.

We all know how difficult it is to exercise authority and power. Either we are too controlling, and want everything to be in order, inhibiting people, or not permitting them to be empowered, as we try in every way just to hold on to things. Or else we run away: We do nothing. We want to be popular and want everyone to love us, so we don't make decisions. And we hurt people by making the decision to not make decisions.

Jesus knows that to exercise authority is not easy. He kneels at our feet, saying, "I want you to exercise your authority in love." As a good shepherd who gives his life for his sheep, he exercises authority with tenderness and love, in truth and forgiveness. When Jesus is at our feet by example, he is illustrating for us how to exercise authority—with humility, not from the top of the pedestal, but down close to people, to look them in the eye, call them forth, and empower them—to help them to grow in freedom and truth.

The washing of the feet in John's Gospel is about service, communion, mutual forgiveness, togetherness, and becoming one.

Through the art of footwashing, we learn to build a better world, one foot at a time.

As the notable Augustinian scholar, Tars van Bavel, O.S.A., indicates in his commentary on *The Rule of Augustine*, "this chapter is one of the most characteristically Augustinian, because Augustine offers here a very personal vision of authority and obedience. Almost every thought reflects the personal spirituality of the author."

Augustine's initial experience with a group of friends and relatives was foundational for forming community along the style of the Acts of the Apostles. Posterior communities promoted by Augustine were highly participatory in structure, not based on the then prevalent notion of *abba* (spiritual father) or *amma* (spiritual mother), but rather praepositus or "the one who is put forward" or "brother prior", not standing above or over the others but alongside them.

In Augustinian lifestyle, the prior has a modest role to play since mutual responsibility among the members of the community is called to prevail. The prior is not to be confused with the president of the school or pastor of the parish, whose roles are entirely different. The Augustinian emphasis is on service, not power. By giving witness to an alternative manner of governing ourselves within a highly hierarchical and partisan society, we can encourage local governments and associations to consider incorporating the principles and values that would allow us to build up community.

For Augustine, authority is an act of loving service. A designated authority figure or leader is not placed above others but remains a part of the community, with special responsibilities and duties toward others. Guiding the community toward the fulfillment of the gospel ideals and being an example to others are two of the most important aspects of the role of authority mentioned by Augustine.

Authority in Augustine is more closely aligned with the concept of service than dominance. The principal service the prior offers is to bear the burden of being responsible and calling the members to be responsible as well for the well-being and functioning of the community as a whole. Augustine never considered a title or an office as an honor, but always a burden (like the backpack a soldier had to carry on his back). Rather than at the top, the person with authority is at the base of the community.

No mention is made of spiritual direction as being among the prior's responsibilities, which is not to say that the prior does not play a spiritual role, including that of promoting the spiritual, apostolic, and community dimensions of the members of the community.

Another point to keep in mind is Augustine's observation that the duty of leadership and the threat of danger go hand in hand. All in positions of authority are liable to be tempted to consolidate their own power rather than use their position in the service of the good of others. Augustine recommends countering this temptation to dominance with an ever-growing commitment to go out of ourselves to enter into communion with God, others, and nature, and trying to see things from the point of view of those who have been left out.

Every member, however, must take responsibility for the progress toward these ideals and the discernment of the community's direction. For Augustine, obedience is a shared responsibility, more than a vertical activity between the superior and the community member. It is also a horizontal activity among all the members of the community. We are all fellow servants, all subject to obedience, even though in different ways. Both obedience and authority are extremely important to ensure unity and harmony in the community, fostering the search for God, and prioritizing the common good above personal interests.

Likewise, obedience shows a loving compassion for the leader who bears greater responsibility for the community and a willingness to listen and cooperate for the common good. This certainly shapes our New Testament understanding of authority as countercultural, as proclaimed by Jesus. Such authority remains gentle and humble because it is always perceived as in service to God, whose servants are thereby served.

We are reminded that we are not religious for ourselves but for a better world, to give witness to how things are called to be in the reign of God. We anticipate living in harmony as a beloved community by doing our best to make sure that our structures visibly communicate our values.

In this epoch, when the church is challenging itself to be a more credible witness in the world, we are called to build structures for listening, to systematically embody the four principal characteristics of Catholic social thought.

Attentive listening

In the work of promoting openness and establishing vital interpersonal relationships, as well as building community, an important tool is the use of talents associated with effective communication. Attentive listening is a basic factor at the heart of good communication.

Modern studies indicate that, in general, people do not know how to listen well. Even when invited to listen carefully, research indicates that less than half the message is heard. And most of that is forgotten within eight hours!

Some people think that listening is a method for taking in information, a function basically the same as hearing. This is a dangerous misconception because it leads us to believe that effective listening is instinctive and so we make little effort to develop listening skills.

In this regard, we have the wisdom of Augustine to guide us: "It is with the heart that one speaks and with the heart that one listens" (Sermon 91, 3).

Many people think of the work of listening as though it were as easy as breathing; they do not think of it as important, as long as it takes place easily. But the consequences of not knowing how to listen attentively can be very serious. Listening without paying attention can give rise to unnecessary problems and cause confusion, misinterpretation, shame, timidity, frustration, and the loss of valuable information.

Attentive listening is an ability that can be acquired and developed. Attentive listening can serve to show our respect and attention to others, encouraging them to share. It also helps us to understand the other's viewpoint.

Effective listening is an active, not a passive process. Listening is taking in information while remaining nonjudgmental and empathetic. It involves acknowledging the person who speaks in such a way that invites communication to continue, while also encouraging carrying the person's thoughts one step forward.

Listening often increases self-esteem since it acknowledges the importance you give to the person being listened to. Acknowledgment is a basic, universal, human need. We are more likely to respond positively to a person who meets these needs than to one who does not.

Listening is also a potent force for reducing stress and tension, for teamwork, and a sense of belonging. When someone knows they are talking to a listener instead of someone who sits in judgment, they usually open up more easily, offering ideas and suggestions.

As far as the impact on interpersonal relations is concerned, a speaker is constantly evaluating the listener. When the other person realizes that you are not paying attention to them, they will usually interpret this as a lack of respect for them as a person. In many instances, these others will respond with arguments in self-defense or with silence. Whatever the reaction, this inattentive listening impedes the growth of trust instead of promoting it.

Rather than being a merely passive activity, the art of listening attentively requires effort and discipline. Listening to understand means gathering information without passing judgment on it, accepting the speaker in a way that advances genuine communication, and giving signs that one is listening and understanding and is interested in what is being said.

When someone speaks, they are transmitting their message by more than words; other factors in play are gestures, facial expressions, and tone of voice. These often make known the emotions or feelings behind the words. Listening solely to another's words is like reading the text of a song without knowing the music.

Attentive listening is important for genuine communication. When we listen attentively, we let the speaker know that their opinion has value. Such a demonstration of openness promotes the mutual trust that is needed for genuine harmonious living.

As Pope Francis wrote on the occasion of the Ordinary General Assembly, for the Ceremony Commemorating the Fiftieth Anniversary of the Institution of the Synod of Bishops, October 2015:

> A synodal Church is a Church which listens, which realizes that listening "is more than simply hearing." It is a mutual listening in which everyone has something to learn. The faithful people, the college of bishops, the Bishop of Rome: all listening to each other, and all listening to the Holy Spirit, the "Spirit of truth", in order to know what he "says to the Churches."
>
> Synodality, as a constitutive element of the Church, offers us the most appropriate interpretive framework for understanding the hierarchical ministry itself. Inasmuch as the Church is nothing other than the "journeying together" of God's flock along the paths of history toward the encounter with Christ the Lord, then we understand too that, within the Church, no one can be "raised up" higher than others. On the contrary, in the Church, it is necessary that each person "lower" himself or herself, so as to serve our brothers and sisters along the way.
>
> But in this Church, as in an inverted pyramid, the top is located beneath the base. Consequently, those who exercise authority are called "ministers" because, in the original meaning of the word, they are the least of all. It is in serving the people of God that each bishop becomes, for that portion of the flock entrusted to him, the vicar of that Jesus who at the Last Supper bent down to wash the feet of the Apostles. And in a similar perspective, the successor of Peter is nothing else if not the *servus servorum Dei*.
>
> Let us never forget this! For the disciples of Jesus, yesterday, today and always, the only authority is the authority of service, the only power is the power of the cross.

Our family, our neighborhood association, our local community, and provincial administration can help promote the synodal process as an alternative manner of governance in our neighborhood and in the world.

Here are some suggestions on how we can promote that cause:

- By becoming better listeners
- By creating structures for active listening in all our apostolic ministries and promoting them in our society
- As people who are committed to living an integral ecology, we can promote special attention to those who have been excluded, left out of the process, going the extra mile to invite them in, to reach out to where they find themselves
- Intentionally trying to become more aware of the impact we are having on our world through mindless consumption, scandalous waste of energy, food, water, and other items not universally available
- By living and promoting attitudes of respectful listening to the cry of the planet, taking note of instances of environmental injustice, and rallying support for those who are excluded from the basic benefits of society
- By incorporating the concept of synodality (listening and walking together on our journey toward the reign of God) in our homilies, syllabi, conferences, and activities.

Concluding Exhortation: The Gracious Gift of Fidelity

Nature as Mirror: A Vignette to Situate the Topic of the Final Chapter of *The Rule*

Anyone who is a parent knows the alarming desperation when their infant child suddenly wails and cries in apparent pain, more than discomfort. What's wrong, what hurts, what can I do?

A quick check with a thermometer indicates a fever of 102! The anguish increases, the torment of not knowing what to do, wanting to alleviate what is causing the temperature to rise, a perilous sign of danger.

Shout to the heavens, cry out to God, an urgent call to the doctor, a mad dash to the emergency room; anything to relieve the pain, to calm the turmoil, to cool down the fever, soothe the nerves.

God is that parent, feeling the angst and desperation, wanting to alleviate the pain, knowing that everything is interdependent, aware that human consumption and waste are the major factors in climate warming, aware of the dangers that a rise of only 3 degrees Fahrenheit can mean for the planet and its inhabitants.

I know how out of sorts I feel when my own temperature rises even a few degrees: the sensation of draining energy, aridity of the throat, harsh breathing, lack of appetite, and muscle pain. The symptoms are multiple and concerning. And that's just me, one person, a slight rise in temperature. God feels this intensely, being a loving parent who longs for abundant life for all people and things.

Perhaps this analogy can help us understand what our planet, our common home, must feel as the temperature rises steadily, progressively, critically. We are invited to plant what we hope to reap: a good harvest of plenty for all. We can help heal, make whole, and become holy to the extent that we go out of ourselves to enter into communion with God, others, and nature. The choice is ours; the time is now.

The Rule of Augustine, Chapter 8

48. May the Lord grant that, filled with "longing for spiritual beauty," you will lovingly observe all that has been written here. Live in such a way that you spread abroad "the life-giving aroma of Christ." "Do not be weighed down like slaves under the law, but live as free men under grace."

    This little book is to be read to you once a week. As in a mirror, you will be able to see in it whether there is anything you are neglecting or forgetting. If you find that your actions match what is written here, thank the Lord who is the giver of every good. If, however, a person sees that he has failed in some way, then let him be sorry for what has occurred in the past and be on his guard for what the future will bring. Let his prayer be: "Forgive me my trespasses and lead me not into temptation."

Water is the oldest reflective surface known to humans, serving as a mirror, allowing us to see a reflection of ourselves as we are. Water, like cryptic liquid glass, serves as a cosmic mirror, reflecting all of creation in images of flourishing trees and thirsty animals that come to drink, reflecting the magnificence of an ever-changing water-bearing sky.

Water throughout history and cultures has been considered sacred, the very essence of life. For many, seeing water brings peace. We know that we are blessed with precious water, the gift of a loving and bountiful Creator. Water also reflects the image of the inner-looking eye, allowing us to contemplate the mystery within:

Concluding Exhortation: The Gracious Gift of Fidelity

Who am I? Where do I come from? What is my place and purpose in life? How am I to relate to nature and to others?

We have inherited so much from previous generations, and we have squandered quite a bit as well.

Water is life. And even though 70 percent of the planet's surface is water, 97 percent of that is saltwater. A large part of the remaining 3 percent that is fresh is in the form of snow and glaciers, leaving only about 1 percent available. Overconsumption, instant gratification, the desire to possess more, indifference, and arrogance in the face of want and misery skew God's plan and unbalances all of creation.

We now take a moment to reflect on the gift of water and all of creation in light of Augustine's *Rule*.

This little book is to be read to you once a week. As in a mirror, you will be able to see in it whether there is anything you are neglecting or forgetting.

Augustine encourages us to look regularly into the Gospel and *The Rule*, as in a mirror, to assess how well we are approaching our goals. Thus, we can monitor our progress in the Christian life, a gradual process of ongoing conversion in Christ. Conversion is a lifelong process. Frequent personal and communal evaluations help us focus on our progress on the journey toward God in oneness of mind and heart.

Augustine's words alert us that on our journey as the pilgrim People of God, we cannot be complacent. Regular review of the process can stimulate renewal and strengthen commitment and fervor.

While striving to live in oneness of mind and heart, intent upon God as proposed by Augustine, we are consoled by the affirmation that God gives us the grace we need to succeed. It is this grace, generously given by God, that grants us the freedom to choose to love one another as Jesus loved and reject selfishness in our relationships. Grace gives us the freedom and the responsibility to find God in ourselves and in one another.

Augustine encourages each of us to use *The Rule* as a mirror, a tool to look at yourself, not so much to see what you look like, as to understand the way you act. The outward image says a lot about

Concluding Exhortation: The Gracious Gift of Fidelity

our inner feelings: drained or radiant with vitality; absent-minded or very focused.

As time passes, you can see yourself aging. Do you see yourself growing wiser as well? How do you perceive yourself in the mirror: with contempt, or respect? With hesitancy, or with sympathy? The way you look at yourself says a lot about the way you deal with yourself: negative, neutral, or positive.

Water can be an instrument to reflect on ourselves, to allow us to see better who we are and how we are relating. Water is an ever-more-precious element, much more than a mere commodity. That is also true of each of us: We are of inestimable value. How we treat water can tell us so much about how we appreciate our Creator, ourselves, and others. Everything is interconnected.

Since water is so precious and becoming ever more scarce, what more can we do to preserve and share this essential and life-giving element?

A simple yet significant action we can take, especially those of us who live in the developed world, is to drink water from the tap! Fossil fuels are used to transport bottled water from factories to stores as well as in the production of plastic bottles. That plastic bottle is generally used only once, then disposed of in the landfill or recycled. At the same time, it behooves us to recognize that tap water is incredibly cheaper than the bottled version.

We can avoid buying bottled water! A one-liter bottle of water requires an average of three liters of water to produce and costs many times more than tap water. At gatherings and events, we can encourage those who attend to bring their own reusable receptacle; as hosts, we can provide jugs of fresh water and encourage others to find alternatives to bottled water.

Looking into a mirror brings you into the present moment. You no longer see the child that used to be, nor can you conjure up what you might look like in a few years. You only see how you are at this moment. In his *Rule*, Augustine invites you to look at yourself unashamedly, and with compassionate eyes.

So, when you are looking in the mirror, Augustine is going to ask you a few questions that can help you think about yourself and your relationships: to God, to others, to yourself, and to nature. Are you perhaps neglecting something? Is there something you forgot, or someone you take for granted, whom you treat as an object at your service?

Looking in the mirror leads to self-reflection, to considering your situation. How am I doing? Am I feeling all right? Do I live from my heart? Have I neglected feelings or experiences that are important to me? Have I been attentive to the signals I get from my surroundings? Do I live without thinking of others? Have I forgotten to pay attention to someone who needs me? Have I sufficiently kept my sight on God?

Self-reflection can lead to a healthy critical evaluation. Whenever I realize I have neglected or forgotten someone or something, I can conceive a plan to take better care of the matter in the future. It is advisable to look in the mirror regularly, not only to see your body, but also to look into your inner face.

As mentioned earlier, we propose a methodology with New Testament origins to aid us in the process of continual systematic conversion and growth in living harmony: the *signs of the times methodology*, identified by the three steps or stages that comprise the method: **See—Judge—Act**. This method is more for examination of our communal lifestyle, how our society measures up against the gospel principles, the Beatitudes.

We offer these guidelines for the communal looking in the mirror:

- **See** refers to the point of departure: taking account of our lived reality. We attempt to get a handle on where we are and how we are doing on our way toward living harmony on a broader scale.

- **Judge** refers to what Augustine recommends that we do once a week: examine ourselves, "as in a mirror, you will be able to see in it whether there is anything you are neglecting or forgetting." We hold up before ourselves the ideal, as we understand it, to perceive more clearly how we are living it and in what ways we are being called to grow.

- **Act** refers to identifying the next possible step forward, toward the goal of a life more in harmony with nature, with others, with God, with myself.

From an Augustinian perspective, we entitle this process "Searching Together": a community exercise (done with others, not for others, as a way of respecting their dignity; walking with others; being willing to learn from others).

See: to observe, hear, and experience the lived reality of people and of the community itself.

Seeing goes beyond first impressions, which tend to yield incomplete pictures as they are often influenced by our expectations or assumptions and are based on limited information. The *seeing* portion of our community exploration of an issue or topic is designed to help us face the facts, move beyond a discussion based solely on personal opinions. Social analysis is an effort to obtain a more complete picture of a social situation by exploring its historical and structural relationships. Social analysis also considers who is making decisions affecting people and the values underlying those decisions. Social situations are complex, and our analysis is always limited. Despite that, searching together and sharing our observations can help us see a situation more completely than one based merely on first impressions.

This involves naming what it is that you observe that causes you concern. It means carefully, respectfully, examining the primary data of the situation: What are the people involved doing, feeling, and saying? What is happening to them, and how are they responding?

Some of the questions to be addressed by participants might be:

- What do we know about this situation?
  What are we able to observe about it?
- What specific facts can we cite about
  this experience or issue?
- How do we feel in the face of this issue or experience?

- How does this situation touch me personally?

More emphasis on asking questions, sharing a vision and views on the topic at hand, and listening, can lead to more effective judgments and actions.

Judge or discern: An ethical reflection to actively seek out God's point of view.

The second step, *judging*, is the crux of the matter, and it involves confronting a situation in light of the guiding principles of our life:

- Scripture
- The four basic principles of Catholic Social Teaching
  - Dignity
  - The Common Good
  - Subsidiarity
  - Solidarity

The goal of this step is to begin to formulate a response to a problematic social situation, identifying an area for growth. Our beliefs shape our judgments, and our values can always be better informed by sharing our personal understanding without being either defensive or imposing. This cannot happen without guidance from the Spirit. This means allowing ourselves to benefit from the collective wisdom of the community, past and present, as consensus emerges from our sharing. The wisdom reflects the activity of the Spirit, alive in the community members and in our sharing.

A spiritual discernment, as it turns more practical, will try to take into account all the positive and limiting elements present in each possible activity or direction. That implies that all the members of the community be free enough to examine and consider positive and negative elements. Theory alone will not enable the community to bring about change; we need to consider meaningful actions.

Typically, this step includes prayer, petition for the guidance of the Spirit, to see ourselves and our world as God, the loving and merciful Father does, with compassion, forgiveness, and acceptance; not in an indifferent fashion, or with anger, or envy, or contempt, like the elder son in the parable of the prodigal son.

Act in Charity and Justice: to move forward in God's plan for a fuller life with all of creation.

As a result of the insights from the previous two steps, a decision for social and personal change emerges, a commitment to transform reality. From the information gathered, analyzed, and reflected upon, proposals for concrete actions surface, actions meant to influence and change the situation and address its root causes. Seeing (and sharing our observations) and judging (by listening to what we understand to be God's light on the topic) lead to acting together.

The concepts of charity and justice help distinguish the types of action:

- **Charity** responds to people's immediate needs (food, shelter, safety, and clothing), and tends to flow from a generous, compassionate, or altruistic heart.
- **Justice** seeks to address the causes or reasons why people are without adequate resources; it usually requires long-term collaborative efforts with community members and can involve changing perceptions as well as systems, policies, and institutions.

Charity and justice are not isolated actions and, consequently, our response to any particular situation might very well involve both. Distinguishing between charity and justice can serve as a helpful reminder that each is important and incomplete without the other. Charity might be seen as a starting point for fostering solidarity across social divisions. However, charity without justice can ignore the structural inequalities that provoke the need for charity in the first place or might reinforce unjust relationships.

We need to be cautious to avoid toxic charity, which—though well-intentioned—frequently, although unwittingly, can foster paternalism or foment dependency. Doing good to others or for others rather than doing good *with* them, taking them into account as subjects, not objects, as agents of their own destiny, supporting but not replacing them, is the true task of charity.

One type of justice-oriented service is advocacy, standing alongside, supporting, encouraging, and accompanying others, not taking their place, nor speaking for them rather than on their behalf. Justice-oriented advocacy can involve empowering individuals and communities to create structural change.

The concrete activities we identify need to be practical and possible to accomplish. Ideally, our actions will include:

- A personal commitment (not something for others to do), something specific, as simple as a conversation with someone during the coming week, or raising a particular topic, to influence an attitude. The more specific the action, the greater the chance of actually doing it.

- A communal commitment (something we do together) that enriches our experience of communion, a significant action representing the united commitment of the community. This may take time to identify and establish.

- That our actions be transformational, responding to the "why" question addressing the root causes, while also responding to immediate needs (give a fish, teach how to fish, but ask why some people know how to fish while others don't, why some eat fish in abundance while others have never tasted a fish).

The particularly Augustinian perspective of this entire process, from beginning to end, is embodied in dialogue, the path toward communion, the search together for the truth. Our restless hearts allow us to realize that by respectful dialogue, which includes active listening, we open ourselves to be better able to "discover God in one another, whose temples we have become."

We are more fully alive, more fully human, more closely related to our divine Creator to the extent that we relate to one another. The more we share, the more truly like Christ we become, who shared—and continues to share—his entire self with us. We search together, we share the journey, and we always reach out in ever-broadening concentric circles, building community and a communion of communities.

Allow me to share with you the example of Augustinian Defender of the Rights of the Poor, A.D.R.O.P., which strives to combine charity and justice, accompanied and enriched by the broader community, advocating for transformational change.

In AD 401, Saint Augustine urged the Council of Bishops meeting in Carthage to call on the Roman Emperor to reestablish the office of defender of the rights of the poor.

In 2004, the Province of Saint Thomas of Villanova revived this position and created a structure to promote solidarity, spearheaded by Fr. Jack Deegan, O.S.A., who gathered leaders, service providers, and volunteers together to assess the needs of the poor in South Philadelphia and began to match those needs with known resources.

The Mission of the Augustinian Defenders of the Rights of the Poor is to build bridges between providers, recipients, and community leaders across economic, political, and religious spectra. A.D.R.O.P. accomplishes its mission by matching individuals with identified needs to known resources, to build better communities.

Poverty is rampant today, and the gulf between the rich and the poor is widening. We, as Augustinian religious and committed laypeople, must make awareness of poverty the center of our concern and devote a major portion of our time, talents, and treasure to fostering systemic change in the way poverty is addressed.

A.D.R.O.P. invites educational institutions, parish ministries, and other grassroots organizations to use their expertise to understand the causes of poverty and what can be done to effect real, sustainable change.

One of the several ministries within A.D.R.O.P. is Caritas Populorum, which is designed to respond to the social, economic, health, and educational needs of the people of Peru in conjunction, principally, with the ministries of the Augustinians and the Sisters of Saint Joseph.

Call to Action

Head, heart, and hands (doctrine, spirituality, and pastoral activity), all three are summoned to provide a personal, communal, and transformational response to the current state of affairs. The sum of many, countless small actions, day in and day out, by many different people, is what determines who we all are together. Building a better world passes through the building up of a local community and the coordination among smaller communities to promote living in harmony, guided by the basic principles of Catholic social thought.

The four essential principles of Catholic social thought—dignity, common good, subsidiarity, and solidarity—are not meant to be mere intellectual titillation or solely academic speculation; all four together are tools to confront our reality—the pressing social issues which interrupt God's plan for abundant life to the full for all—to allow the Spirit of God to awaken in us creative responses, involving concrete activities in pursuit of the next possible step toward building a better world for all: social thought to stimulate social action. Augustine's *Rule*, with its centuries of adherents, has much to offer in the line of pushing us on to the horizon.

Pope Francis encouraged us to act personally and communally:

> Local individuals and groups can make a real difference. They are able to instill a greater sense of responsibility, a strong sense of community, a readiness to protect others, a spirit of creativity and a deep love for the land. (*Laudato si'*, no. 179)

> All Christian communities have an important role to play in ecological education (*Laudato si'*, no. 214)

Call to Action

In speeches and interviews, Pope Leo XIV has raised concern over the unchecked growth of technological development and market-driven environmental harm. He warns that profit motives, when left unregulated, often drive decisions that damage creation and deepen inequality.

Pope Leo is not dismissing science or innovation out of hand. He has also noted the benefits to humanity that technology and innovation can bring. Instead, he is saying that their development should be "disciplined by justice, guided by wisdom, and tethered to the common good." This line of critique echoes Catholic teaching while also aligning with secular calls for stronger climate regulation, sustainable tech design, and corporate accountability.

One of Pope Leo's first acts as pope was to declare that the world is in a "global climate emergency," urging leaders to "move from words to action." He has pressed fossil fuel companies to transition their portfolios and publicly endorsed clean energy investment.

"Symbolism is not enough," Pope Leo said. "To be stewards of the Earth, we must be accountable in our choices—starting with our own."

Instead, Pope Leo advocates a "relationship of reciprocity" with the natural world. Quoting Genesis, he often reminds audiences that dominion over creation does not mean exploitation but rather care and responsibility.

Pope Leo sees no daylight between environmental degradation and inequality. Integral ecology focuses our attention on both the cry of the planet and that of the poor. They are intimately related, absolutely interdependent. Pollution, water scarcity, and climate-driven disasters disproportionately affect the poor. As such, Pope Leo has spoken out about the moral imperative to link environmental policy with anti-poverty measures, stating that the Earth is not ours to waste, but a gift given for the benefit of all.

This holistic approach aligns closely with today's global environmental justice movement, which centers the needs and experiences of frontline communities. By rooting these goals in Catholic theology, Pope Leo offers a powerful bridge between faith traditions and modern environmental advocacy. His message is resonating across those schools of thought.

In Pope Leo's message prepared for the 9th World Day of the Poor (November 16, 2025), we find this summary inspired by Augustine's commitment to discover and attend to Christ among us:

> In this promotion of the common good, our social responsibility is grounded in God's creative act, which gives everyone a share in the goods of the earth. Like those goods, the fruits of human labor should be equally accessible to all. Helping the poor is a matter of justice before a question of charity. As Saint Augustine observed: "You give bread to a hungry person; but it would be better if none were hungry, so that you would have no need to give it away. You clothe the naked, but would that all were clothed and that there be no need for supply this lack" (*In I Ioan.*, 8:5).
>
> It is my hope, then, that this Jubilee Year will encourage the development of policies aimed at combatting forms of poverty both old and new, as well as implementing new initiatives to support and assist the poorest of the poor. Labor, education, housing and health are the foundations of a security that will never be attained by the use of arms. I express my appreciation for those initiatives that already exist, and for the efforts demonstrated daily on the international level by great numbers of men and women of good will.

Recently, Pope Leo encouraged us: "Do not hesitate to share the joy and the amazement born of your contemplation of the "seeds" that, in the words of Saint Augustine, God has sown in the harmony of the universe" (cf. *De Genesis ad Litteram*, V, 23, 44-45). This phrase of Augustine refers to the idea that God created the world with fundamental principles and potential for order and beauty, much like a gardener plants seeds that will grow into a thriving garden. These "seeds" represent the inherent capacity for good,

Call to Action

harmony, and beauty within the universe, including within human beings. The phrase emphasizes the importance of sharing the awe and amazement that comes from contemplating God's creation with others, fostering a sense of unity and shared purpose.

The pursuit of knowledge and understanding, inspired by these divine "seeds," can lead to a more peaceful and just world, in which all parts of creation are interconnected and contribute to the overall beauty and order of the universe, and in which we all learn to live in harmony.

Appendix

THE RULE OF SAINT AUGUSTINE: living in harmony, being of one mind and heart on the way to God.

Opening Exhortation

1. We urge you who form a religious community to put the following precepts into practice.

2. Before all else, brothers, we must love God and our neighbor because these are the greatest commandments.

Chapter 1

3. Before all else, live together in harmony, being of one mind and one heart on the way to God. For is it not precisely for this reason that you have come to live together?

4. Among you, there can be no question of personal property. Rather, take care that you share everything in common. Your superior should see to it that each person is provided with food and clothing. He does not have to give exactly the same to everyone, for you are not all equally strong, but each person should be given what he personally needs. For this is what you read in the Acts of the Apostles: "Everything they owned was held in common, and each one received whatever he had need of" (4:32, 35).

Appendix

5. Those who owned possessions in the world should readily agree that, from the moment they enter the religious life, these become the property of the community.

6. Those who did not have possessions ought not to strive in the religious community for what they could not obtain outside of it. One must have, indeed, regard for their frailty by providing for them whatever they need, even if they were formerly so poor that they could not even afford the necessities of life. They may not, however, consider themselves fortunate because they now receive food and clothing, which were beyond their means in earlier years.

7. Nor should they give themselves airs because they now find themselves in the company of people whom they would not have ventured to approach before. Their heart should seek for nobler things, not vain earthly appearance. If, in their religious life, rich people were to become humble and the poor people haughty, then this style of life would seem to be of value only to the rich and not to the poor.

8. On the other hand, let those who appear to have had some standing in the world not look down upon their brothers who have entered the religious community from a condition of poverty. They ought to be more mindful of their life together with poor brothers than of the social status of their wealthy parents. And the fact that they have made some of their possessions available to the community gives them no reason to have a high opinion of themselves. Otherwise, people would more easily fall prey to pride in sharing riches with the community than they would have done if they had enjoyed them in the world. For while all vices manifest themselves in wrongdoing, pride lurks also in our good works, seeking to destroy even them. What good does it do to distribute one's possessions to the poor and to become poor oneself, if giving up riches makes the person prouder than he was when he had a fortune?

9. You are all to live together, therefore, "one in mind and one in heart," and honor God in one another because each of you has become his temple.

Chapter 2

10. "Persevere faithfully in prayer" at the hours and times appointed.

11. The place of prayer should not be used for any purpose other than that for which it is intended and from which it takes its name. Thus, if someone wants to pray there, even outside the appointed hours, in his own free time, he should be able to do so without being hindered by others who have no business being there.

12. When you pray to God in psalms and songs, the words spoken by your lips should also be alive in [your] heart.

13. When you sing, keep to the text you have, and [do] not sing what is not intended to be sung.

Chapter 3

14. As far as your health allows, keep your bodily appetites in check by fasting and abstinence from food and drink. Those who are unable to fast the whole day may have something to eat before the main meal, which takes place in the late afternoon. They may do this, however, only around midday. But the sick may have something to eat any time of day.

15. From the beginning of the meal to the end, listen to the customary reading without noise or protest against Scriptures, for you have not only to satisfy your physical hunger, but also "to hunger for the Word of God."

16. There are some who are weaker because of their former manner of life. If an exception is made for them at table, those who are

stronger because they have come from a different way of life ought not to take this amiss or to consider it unfair. They should not think that the others are more fortunate because they are capable of something [that] is beyond the strength of the others.

17. There are some who, before entering the religious life, were accustomed to living comfortably, and therefore they have received something more in the way of food and clothing: better bedding perhaps, or more blankets. The others who are stronger, and therefore happier, do not receive these things. But, taking into account the former habits of life of the rich, keep in mind how much they now have to do without, even though they cannot live as simply as those who are physically stronger. Not everyone should want to have the extra he sees another receive, for this is done not to show favor but only out of concern for the person. Otherwise, deplorable disorder would creep into religious life, whereby the poor begin to drift easily along while the rich put themselves out in every possible way.

18. The sick should obviously receive suitable food, otherwise, their illness would only get worse. Once they are over the worst of their sickness, they ought to be well cared for so that they may be fully restored to health as quickly as possible. And this holds good even if they formerly belonged to the very poorest class in society. During their convalescence, they should receive the same care that the rich are entitled to because of their former manner of life. But once they have made a complete recovery, they are to go back to living as they did earlier on, when they were happier because their needs were fewer. The simpler [the] way of life, the better it is suited to servants of God.

Chapter 4

19. Do not attract attention by the way [you] dress. Endeavor to impress by your manner of life, not by the clothes you wear.

Appendix

20. When you go out, go with somebody else, and stay together when you have reached your destination.

21. Whatever you are doing, your behavior should in no way cause offense to anyone, but should rather be in keeping with the holiness of your way of life.

22. When you see a woman, do not keep provocatively looking at her. Of course, no one can forbid you to see women when you go out, "but it is wrong to desire a woman or to want her to desire you." For it is not only by affectionate embraces that desire between man and woman is awakened, but also by looks. You cannot say that your inner attitude is good if, with your eyes, you desire to possess a woman; for the eye is the herald of the heart. And if people allow their impure intentions to appear, albeit without words, but just looking at each other and finding pleasure in each other's passion, even though not in each other's arms, we cannot speak any longer of true chastity, which is precisely that of the heart.

23. Indeed, if a person cannot keep his eyes off of a woman and enjoys attracting her attention, he should not imagine that others do not see this. Of course, they see it, even people [who] you would not expect to notice it. But even if it did remain concealed and unseen by men, will it not be seen by "God who scans the heart of every man" and from whom nothing is hidden? Or are we to imagine that "God does not see it" because just as his wisdom is far beyond ours, so too is he prepared to be extraordinarily patient with us? A religious should be afraid "to offend the God of love," and for the sake of this love, he ought to be ready to give up a sinful love for a woman. Whoever is mindful that God sees all things will not wish to look at a woman with sinful desire. For, precisely on this point, the text of Scripture, "the Lord abhors a covetous eye," impresses on us that we are to stand in awe of him.

24. Therefore, in church or wherever you may be in the company of women, you are to consider yourselves responsible for one

Appendix

another's chastity. Then "God who dwells in you" will watch over you through your responsibility for one another.

25. If you notice in a brother this provocative look I have spoken of, then warn him immediately, so that the evil that has taken root may not worsen and so that he may promptly improve his behavior.

26. If, after this admonition, you see him doing the same thing again, anyone who notices it should consider him a sick person in need of treatment. At that time, nobody is any longer free to be silent. "First inform one or two others of the situation so that with two or three you will be able to convince him of his fault," and to call him to order with due firmness. Do not think that you are acting out of ill will in doing this. On the contrary, you would be at fault if, by your silence, you allow your brothers to meet their downfall, when by speaking you could set them on the right path.

27. If he does not wish to listen to your warning, then first advise the superior so that he and the brother may talk the matter out in private, and in this way, others will not need to know of it or be involved. If he is still unwilling to listen, then you may bring in others to convince him of his fault. If he still persists in denying it, then, without his knowledge, others must be brought in, so that "his faults may be pointed out" to him "by more than a single witness in the presence of all," for the word of two or three witnesses is more [convincing] than that of one.

Once his guilt has been established, it is up to the superior or even to the priest under whose jurisdiction the religious house falls, to determine which punishment he should best undergo with a view to his improvement. If he refuses to submit to this punishment, he is to be sent away from the community, even though he himself may be unwilling to go. Here again, this action is not to be prompted by heartlessness but by love, for in this way he is prevented from having a bad influence on others and contributing to their downfall, too.

Appendix

28. What I have said about looking at a woman lustfully holds too for other sins. In discovering, warding off, bringing to light, proving, and punishing all other faults, you are faithfully and diligently to follow the procedure set out above, always with love for the people involved but with aversion for their faults.

29. If a brother, of his own accord, confesses that he has gone so far along the wrong path as to receive letters and gifts secretly from a woman, we ought to deal with him gently and pray for him. But if he is found out and proved guilty, he is to be severely punished according to the judgment of the priest or superior.

Chapter 5

30. Your clothes should be looked after in common by one or more brothers who are to see that they are well aired and kept free from moths. Just as the food you eat is prepared in the one kitchen, so the clothes you wear are to come from the one storeroom.

    And as far as possible, it should not matter to you greatly which summer or winter clothes you receive. It does not make any difference whether you get back the same clothes you handed in or something that has been worn by another, "provided no one is denied what he needs." If this gives rise to jealousy or grumbling, or if people begin complaining that the clothes they now have are not as good as those they had before, or if they think it beneath them to wear clothes that had previously been worn by others, does that not tell you something? If the external matter of dress becomes a cause of discord, does this not prove that inwardly, in the attitude of your heart, there is something sadly lacking? But if you are unable to do these things and your weakness is taken into consideration so that you are allowed to receive again the same clothes you handed in, even so, keep them all in the one place where they will be looked after by those charged with this task.

31. The intention behind all this is that no one will seek his own advantage in his work. Everything you do is to be for the service

of the community, and you are to work with more zeal and enthusiasm than if each person were merely working for himself and his own interests. For it is written of love that "it is not self-seeking"; that is to say, love puts the interests of the community before personal advantage, and not the other way around. Therefore, the degree to which you are concerned for the interests of the community rather than your own is the criterion by which you can judge how much progress you have made. Thus, in all the fleeting necessities of human life, "something sublime and permanent" reveals itself, "namely love."

32. It follows from this that a religious who receives clothes or other useful items from his parents or relatives may not keep these quietly for himself. He should place them at the disposal of the superior. "Once they have become the property of the community, it is up to the superior to see that these articles find their way into the hands of those who need them." But should anyone conceal a gift he has received, he shall be judged guilty of theft.

33. When you want to wash your clothes or have them washed at a laundry, let this take place in consultation with the superior, lest desire for clean clothes sully your character.

34. Because bathing may be necessary for good health, the opportunity to visit the public baths may never be refused. In this matter, follow medical advice without grumbling. Even if a person is unwilling, he shall do what has to be done for the good of his health, if necessary at the command of the superior. But if someone wants to go bathing just because he enjoys it when it is not really necessary, he will have to learn to renounce his desires. For, what a person likes may not always be good for him. It may even be harmful.

35. In any case, if a brother says that he does not feel well, even though he is not noticeably sick, believe him without hesitation. But if you are not sure whether the treatment he wishes to have will be of any benefit to him, then consult a doctor about it.

Appendix

36. See to it that there are always two or more of you when you visit the public baths. Indeed, this applies wherever you go. And it is not for you to choose the people who will go with you—you are to leave this to the decision of the superior.

37. Someone should be deputed by the community to care for the sick. At the same time, the person ought to take care of those who are convalescing and those who are weak, even though they are not running a temperature. The infirmarian may take from the kitchen whatever he himself considers necessary.

38. Those responsible for food, clothes, and books should serve their brothers without grumbling.

39. Books will be available every day at the appointed hour, and not at any other time.

40. The brothers in charge of clothes and shoes should not delay in making these available to those who need them.

Chapter 6

41. Do not quarrel. But if you do have a quarrel, put an end to it as quickly as possible. Otherwise, an isolated moment of anger grows into hatred, "the splinter becomes a beam," and you make your heart a murderer's den. For we read in the Scriptures: "Whoever hates his brother is a murderer."

42. If you have hurt a person by abusing him, or by cursing or grossly accusing him, be careful to make amends for the harm you have done, as quickly as possible, by apologizing to him. And the one who has been hurt should be ready in his turn to forgive you without wrangling. Brothers who have insulted each other should "forgive each other's trespasses." If you fail to do this, your praying the Our Father becomes a lie. Indeed, the more you pray, the more honest your prayer ought to become.

   It is better to have to deal with a person who, though quick to anger, immediately seeks a reconciliation once he realizes he has been unjust to another, than with someone who is less easily roused, but also less inclined to seek forgiveness. But "a person who never wants to ask forgiveness, or who fails to do so from the heart," does not belong in the religious community, even though he may not be sent away.

Be cautious of hard words. Should you utter them, then do not be afraid to speak the healing word with the same mouth that caused the wound.

43. From time to time, the necessity of keeping order may compel you to use harsh words to the young people who have not yet reached adulthood, in order to keep them in line. In that case, you are not required to apologize, even though you yourself consider that you have gone too far. For if you are too humble and submissive in your conduct toward these young people, then your authority, which they should be ready to accept, will be undermined. In such cases, you should ask the forgiveness from the Lord of all, who knows with what deep affection you love your brothers, even those you might happen to have reproved with undue severity. Do not let love for one another remain caught up in self-love; rather, such love must be guided by the Spirit.

Chapter 7

44. "Obey your superior" as a father, but also give him due respect on account of his office; otherwise, you offend God in him. This is even more true [of] the priest who bears responsibility for you all.

45. It is primarily up to the superior to see that all that has been said here is put into practice and that infringements are not carelessly overlooked. It is his duty to point out the abuses and to correct them. If something is beyond his competence and power, he should put the matter before the priest, whose authority in some respects is greater than his own.

Appendix

46. Your superior must not think himself fortunate in "having power to lord it over you," but in "the love with which he will serve you." Because of your esteem for him he shall be superior to you; because of his responsibility to God, he shall realize that he is the very least of all the brethren. "Let him show himself an example to all in good work; he is to reprimand those who neglect their work, to give courage to those who are disheartened, to support the weak and to be patient with everyone." He should himself observe the norms of the community and so lead others to respect them too. And let him strive to be loved by you rather than to be feared, although both love and respect are necessary. He should remember that "he is responsible to God for you."

47. By your ready and loving obedience, therefore, you not only "show compassion to yourselves," but also to your superior. For it applies to you as well that the higher the position a person holds, the greater the danger he is in.

Chapter 8

48. May the Lord grant that, filled with "longing for spiritual beauty," you will lovingly observe all that has been written here. Live in such a way that you spread abroad "the life-giving aroma of Christ." Do not be weighed down like slaves under the law, but live as free men under grace.

    This little book is to be read to you once a week. "As in a mirror, you will be able to see in it whether there is anything you are neglecting or forgetting." If you find that your actions match what is written here, thank the Lord who is the giver of every good. If, however, a person sees that he has failed in some way, then let him be sorry for what has occurred in the past and be on his guard for what the future will bring. Let his prayer be: "Forgive me my trespasses and lead me not into temptation."

FOCOLARE MEDIA
Enkindling the Spirit of Unity

The New City Press book you are holding in your hands is one of the many resources produced by Focolare Media, which is a ministry of the Focolare Movement in North America. The Focolare is a worldwide community of people who feel called to bring about the realization of Jesus' prayer: "That all may be one" (see John 17:21).

Focolare Media wants to be your primary resource for connecting with people, ideas, and practices that build unity. Our mission is to provide content that empowers people to grow spiritually, improve relationships, engage in dialogue, and foster collaboration within the Church and throughout society.

 Visit www.focolaremedia.com to learn more about all of New City Press's books, our award-winning magazine *Living City*, videos, podcasts, events, and free resources.

www.ingramcontent.com/pod-product-compliance
Lightning Source LLC
Chambersburg PA
CBHW021007090426
42738CB00007B/688